Whimsical Elegance

Helen Cohen

The Costumed Cat Dolls of Helen Cohen

Photographs by David Gehosky

Schiffer Publishing Ltd
4880 Lower Valley Road • Atglen, PA 19310

Schiffer Books are available at special discounts for bulk purchases for sales promotions or premiums. Special editions, including personalized covers, corporate imprints, and excerpts can be created in large quantities for special needs. For more information contact the publisher:

Published by Schiffer Publishing Ltd.
4880 Lower Valley Road
Atglen, PA 19310
Phone: (610) 593-1777; Fax: (610) 593-2002
E-mail: Info@schifferbooks.com

For the largest selection of fine reference books on this and related subjects, please visit our website at **www.schifferbooks.com**
We are always looking for people to write books on new and related subjects. If you have an idea for a book, please contact us at
proposals@schifferbooks.com

This book may be purchased from the publisher.
Please try your bookstore first.
You may write for a free catalog.

In Europe, Schiffer books are distributed by
Bushwood Books
6 Marksbury Ave.
Kew Gardens
Surrey TW9 4JF England
Phone: 44 (0) 20 8392 8585; Fax: 44 (0) 20 8392 9876
E-mail: info@bushwoodbooks.co.uk
Website: www.bushwoodbooks.co.uk

All text and concepts by author
Photography by David Gehosky

Library of Congress Control Number: 2012933388

Designed by RoS
Type set in Bernhard Tango Swash/Schneidler Md BT
ISBN: 978-0-7643-4099-4
Printed in China

Dedication

To my family — each and every one.

Acknowledgments

Thanks to my husband, Gene, for stressing the importance of making every effort to write without the "passive voice."

Contents

Introduction

Background

I have loved dolls for as long as I can remember, and I played with them probably long after other girls had given them up. As a child, I learned to sew my first primitive doll clothes on my mother's treadle sewing machine. Once I was grown, I sewed my own clothes, and fell in love with all things fashion related. After graduating college, I earned a Master's degree in Social Work, but continued to spend my free time on sewing, knitting, embroidery, or appliqué work.

My evolution as a self-taught doll artist and historical costume enthusiast began over forty years ago, while at home following the birth of the first of my two sons. I began crafting what we used to call Rag Dolls, and for several years both created and sold countless numbers of them through shops, to friends, and at shows. My product range included traditional dolls, outfitted animals I made of imitation fur, plus separate clothing for commercially made dolls. Most importantly, however, through those years of constant experimentation coupled with persistent trial and error, I developed invaluable and essential doll-making skills, such as tight stuffing techniques, pattern making, hair styling, and working with every conceivable kind of fabric. In retrospect, I see how the development of these proficiencies laid the groundwork for where I am now as a doll artist.

I very much wanted to expand my creative endeavors; that is, discover a way of combining love of fashion with dressing a sophisticated adult figure in beautiful costumes with spectacular fabrics. There were no appropriate undressed dolls on the market, no classes that I knew of, and as I had no formal art training, whatsoever, I was on my own. There were precious few how-to books on doll-making at that time, but my breakthrough moment came with the discovery of a slim British book (unfortunately, now long lost), on how to make 16" tall dolls of adult proportions with three-dimensional felt faces and wire armature. An armature is, essentially, the skeleton or foundation upon which one builds the body to the desired shape and, in the case of historical costuming, to create the appropriate outline or silhouette. The wire structure provides the needed flexibility to place the doll and limbs in virtually any body position. An artist friend taught me how to sculpt a porcelain face, a more realistic alternative to felt.

When I first began replicating historical fashion onto my doll figures, I was nothing if not a purist. I began by focusing on British historical costume, and, unabashedly, on fashion worn by the wealthy. I was born in England, and although I came to America as a child, I retain a soft spot for the land of my birth and, yes, of Royalty. I spent hours upon hours at university libraries, where I could access the stacks, but could not borrow the reference books. With each new fashion project, and in the interest of accuracy, I researched everything down to the minutest detail, from dress color to the cut of a bodice seam. All the dolls wore correct undergarments, and where appropriate, wired understructures. Although not visible to the viewer, *I* knew they were there. I even went so far as to use only pure fiber fabrics (no synthetics).

Although I had a professional degree and worked in my field, my passion for creating with my hands and the need to express myself artistically remained, frankly, a far more powerful force in my life. In 1977, I happily gave up social work and opened a retail store, The Doll Lady, which I operated for twenty-two years, first in Yardley and then in Newtown, Pennsylvania. I thought I would sell primarily dolls, including my own rag dolls, but the emphasis quickly changed to dollhouses and miniatures, which was fast becoming an extremely popular, nation-wide hobby.

As the focus of the shop shifted to miniatures, my artistic journey moved into another dimension, literally! All those years of honing doll-making skills, along with my continuing costume research, were put to good use in a new world where everything was 1" to 1' scale. Everything in the real world that is one foot becomes one inch in miniature; for example, a lady figure is roughly five and one half inches. Challenged to distill historical fashion to the essentials of a time period, I soon discovered that these tinier costumes translated onto the doll in a markedly different manner from their larger counterparts. I needed to sharpen my understanding of the inherent properties of fabric, scale of trim, and how to avoid the dreaded bulk that can doom a costume.

During the time of my shop's existence, I established a solid reputation in the miniature business and sold hundreds of dolls. In 1981, twenty of my miniature dolls, including men, ladies, and children were on display in a custom-made dollhouse at The White House during the Christmas season. Over the years, numerous articles on my work appeared in newspapers, national miniature magazines, and the *Doll Reader*. I established two lines of miniature dolls available for sale: those dressed in silks with more costly trims, and an entire separate line of lower priced dolls, dressed in cotton fabrics, which I wholesaled to other miniature shops for resale. All the dolls wore historically accurate clothing and hairstyles.

By the time I closed my shop in 1999, I was ready for a new adventure. I returned to the larger-size figure, where I can, simultaneously, indulge my love of sumptuous fabrics and also delve into far more intricate detail and embellishment, which are now essential hallmarks of my work. Each doll takes a considerable amount of time to complete, and prolonged concentration on one outfit or theme at a time presents me with a vicarious opportunity to step into another time zone – onto a kind of sartorial and theatrical catwalk.

Why Cats?

I am sure the reader is wondering how and why I choose to use cat instead of human faces. Quite simply, I am combining my three loves: dolls, costumes, and cats. A friend once aptly said:

Cats Are Living Sculpture.

Composing a human body with a cat face provides me with inspiration, while stimulating the imagination and personal creativity. The combined figure of a popular animal with a sophisticated body from another species, attired in splendid and richly adorned clothing, takes the viewer to a different philosophical dimension. Do we see an animal or a person, or do the two morph into each other? I do not profess to have an answer: I just love the combination!

Using cat instead of human faces presents an interesting challenge. I have no doubt that we owners project onto our pet a range of thoughts and feelings, certain that we know what our cat is really thinking. Cats, however, are not able to show facial expressions in the same way as we do, and humans rely heavily on the face to communicate with each other. Therefore, body language, through stance, posture, gesture, and/or tilt of the head, is often the compensatory tool for imparting the desired message. Many of the dolls' names incorporate wordplay, thereby, adding to their whimsy and quirky elegance.

I need to point out that the one thing I do not do, myself, is make the cats' heads. When I learned how to make the china faces for my fashion dolls, I recognized that I do not enjoy sculpting at all, and sensed that I would not be very good at it. A deep passion for costuming, and my skills in working with textiles, are where I choose to place my artistic emphasis. Indeed, sculpting and costuming are two very different skill sets and interests. I suspect that many doll artists favor one over the other. The majority of the cats' heads come from a company, called Conversation Concepts, located in Fitchburg, Massachusetts, which sells to multiple retail businesses. The resin faces have excellent detail and are very realistic, but I apply my own personal mark on every one by painting over all or part of the surface. For whiskers, I use those that drop naturally from my real cat, Gwendolyn.

Why This Book?

My audience for this book is many fold: cat fanciers, doll makers, historical fashion enthusiasts, theater costume designers, students of photography, and any one who appreciates a beautiful book to keep on a coffee table.

Although very talented artists have fashioned clothed dolls with animal heads, I know of no book depicting an entire collection of them, or of any that addresses one specific animal; in this case, cats. Above all, the book's uniqueness resides in its focus on dolls presented in accurate historical fashions. Even among my few fantasy creations, the initial inspiration for each figure's costume originates with a historical time line, ranging from the 1500s to 1920. Explanations indicate when a costume is a faithful reproduction of an era, a loose translation, or an adventure into fantasy. In each of their descriptions, I explain what I am trying to achieve through the various uses of fabrics, colors, and trims. I describe not only fashion specifics, but also how the costumer can add lavish applications of detailed adornment and embellishments, but still maintain the ensemble's essential character. For me, this step injects theatricality and invention, both of which, as an artist, I find very exciting. The concepts can be applied to dolls of all sizes, puppets, marionettes, stuffed animals, and full-sized costuming, Where it can be helpful to put into a larger historical context, I add factual information.

Many volumes and manuals exist on the subject of fashion. In the Selected Bibliography, I list those I used most frequently, but not exclusively, when needing to confirm costume details for this book. They represent only a small portion of my personal library, and I suggest further reading for anyone interested in pursuing the topic. The books contain detailed information by authorities on costume who have spent their lives researching and examining every aspect of clothing, so that amateurs like me can learn from them. Making no claim to be an expert, I am a long-standing devotee of absolutely anything having to do with costume and fashion, with particular emphasis on British history.

While I share a generous number of my favorite tips, tricks, and discoveries, I did not design this book as a top-to-bottom primer on doll making. The books on that subject, which I find particularly useful and comprehensive, are those by artist and doll maker, Susanna Oroyan. She is, sadly, no longer alive, but her books are still in print.

I plan to keep the thirty-one dolls featured here in the family; however, by showcasing them in this book, I am fortunate in being able to share them pictorially with a large spectrum of people who share my interests.

Several points of information about the texts in each chapter; whenever I refer to a doll by its name, it appears in Capital Letters. All words appearing in quotations are described in the Glossary of Terms, while anything in italics refer to special meanings, or words of emphasis. In the Table of Contents, I list all the figures in alphabetical order, with a subheading of the fashion's historical origin.

It's All in the Presentation!

Do we not all engage in some form of personal presentation? We live in a culture that places great value on outward appearance. With the arrival into the world of my grandchildren, I was suddenly struck by the fact that we immediately cover their tiny bodies, already at birth, with all manner of outfits, one more adorable than the next. As we mature, we make our own clothing decisions, developing an individual style, but basically, within the parameters of what society considers attractive. Attempting to put into words my almost life-long fascination with costume and historical fashion, I cannot help but conclude that theater and drama play integral parts in our outward presentation, whether intentionally or not. Every era had its own preferences and dictates for ideal feminine and masculine beauty, which to our contemporary eyes might seem peculiar. For example, during much of the first half of the seventeenth century, exposure of the lower part of a lady's arm was viewed as more sexually provocative than highly visible bare breasts nearly tumbling out of a low cut bodice. Or, during the relatively demure fashion we associate with the time of Jane Austen, to expose an ankle was considered shockingly alluring. The bits of pantalettes peeking out below almost ankle-length skirts, generally only went to the knee, where they were tied to the leg – all in the name of outward presentation, not hygiene.

Just as costumers must be cognizant of clothing's historical basics, much the same is required of doll-makers who aspire to represent accurate fashion. One can choose to reproduce a fashion literally in exact detail or through detours, employing imagination and fantasy. In either case, I cannot emphasize enough the importance of a grasp, not only of the specific fashion in question, but also of the all-important fashion silhouette, which telegraphed the idealized look of the time. I make frequent reference to silhouettes in the descriptive doll texts, as it is through the body's outline, much of it achieved by spectacular corsetry, that a costume becomes immediately recognizable and identifiable. The dolls' elegant clothing reflects the height of style that the well-to-do or Royalty would conceivably wear. As portrayed in fashion plates, paintings, periodicals, and drawings, the depictions aspire to represent, in essence, an ideal of contemporary fashion.

How I Approach a New Doll

I am often asked if I draw or sketch out the costume before beginning my work. The answer is I do not. I conceptualize in three dimension; therefore, flat drawing does not help me visualize. Further, by not mapping out the particulars in advance, I allow myself the freedom to shift gears as the doll evolves. Doll making provides unending rewards and artistic challenges. Perhaps the greatest of them rests in the constant invention of new strategies and methods for meeting design requirements to fulfill the chosen concept. I keep a notebook with any and all ideas that occur to me, listing them by potential theme or titles, often with whimsical names. Having selected the appropriate cat's face, I turn to my library of fashion books to determine which historical period best brings my inspiration to life. The next question to answer is: What will the doll do? Will it sit or stand, what direction will it look? What will the arms and legs do? Will the hands hold something? Will shoes be visible? Depending on the answers, I construct the body accordingly, taking into consideration that the eventual clothing must conform to the necessary silhouette. Unlike my earlier dolls, I no longer feel the need to apply the same rigid standards to those doll parts the viewer cannot see. Consequently, if a skirt falls to the floor, covering the shoes, I may use a rigid cone shape for the lower body instead of legs. Bustles, for example, can present a perfectly accurate foundation when made of cardboard bent into the right shape. To my mind, it is enough if the viewer can assume the anatomy and undergarments are there. Presentation through illusion.

As with anyone who works with textiles, I have my stash of fabrics, trims, laces, and accouterments of all kinds. I spend a good deal of time in considering different combinations before settling on the most suitable. Regardless of how sure I think I am, I always give that one extra look in fabric and trim stores, lest I might have overlooked a possibility that could add to the finished presentation. If in doubt, I purchase anyway – in case. Besides, I won't remember where I saw it, if and when I decide I need it at a later point. I need to surround myself with a generous number of choices, ranging from definite to maybe. If they are not at my fingertips, I feel creatively restricted.

Once the body is complete and I am satisfied with the painted facial expression, I begin work on the hair and headdress. Almost anything can be transformed into a hairstyle, among the many possibilities; yarn, ribbon, feathers, imitation fur, lace, straw, strung beads, shredded paper, fabric strips, and traditional doll hair, including synthetic viscose to animal fur. Paper toweling is excellent for making clothing patterns. It mimics fabric, lends itself to draping while, simultaneously, allows for adjustments through rips, cuts, and even minor stretching. I do not use a sewing machine in assembling the garments, and they are permanently attached to the bodies. More specific details describing my approaches to costume particulars, appear in the individual texts that follow.

Intuition and instinct are both essential ingredients in the creative process. You may not be able to put it into words, but as you edit each step along your artistic journey, train yourself to listen to that sixth sense of what does and does not work. If it feels off, it probably is: Try something else! I cannot count the number of times I start off in one direction, and find myself pursuing a very different one. The results, more often than not, reveal delightfully exciting surprises and unexpected outcomes.

A Few Words About Fabrics

The tactile, almost sensuous fabrics, now on the market, present the costumer with a cornucopia of excellent options, regardless of whether they are of cotton, velour, silk, or polyester. Silks, especially the Dupioni and taffeta varieties, which I use frequently, contain very special properties. How a silk garment falls and drapes, while still holding its desired shape is, to my mind, unique, and sets the standard against which to evaluate other fabrics: In short, I am describing the manner in which a fabric behaves. That being said, synthetic mixes are perfectly acceptable so long as they behave as silks; at the end of the day, how a textile responds to the costume designer's needs, is crucial in realizing the best presentation. I literally play with my fabrics to discover their secrets. Sometimes, it is a simple matter of turning the material sideways when cutting, so that the selvages are at top and bottom instead of the originally intended side to side. This little trick can significantly change the way a skirt gathers and falls, especially when dealing with doll-size measurements. Folds, layering, and draping must be logical to the eye and brain in order to be realistic – as if the pull of gravity has a hand in the final result. Consider the option of using the back, or what we call the wrong side, of the fabric as well. No less important is the overall impression of weight: If the fabric looks either too heavy or too flimsy, it is! Use something else.

Scale of design or pattern is another important consideration in making the right selection. For example, a would-love-to-use pattern may be too large when lying flat, but as soon as you take it in hand and introduce gathers, pleats, or draping, you may magically obscure the offending size. With this treatment, it is possible to communicate both the colors and the sense of the design without it seeming out of scale. Conversely, a favored design may actually be too small. Try, instead, to incorporate it as a trim, binding, or edging, against a solid or even a harmonious larger pattern. Just because, at first blush, a fabric may seem inappropriate or counterintuitive does not mean it is out of the question.

The Photographs

If ever there were a perfect example of serendipity, it would have to be in my meeting professional photographer, David Gehosky. A few years ago, the retirement community, where my husband and I reside, hired David to photograph some of the residents and, thankfully, I was one of them, although I almost did not make it to the appointment, as I was running late. I had begun to consider putting this book together, and knew the whole project rested on my finding a perfect fit in selecting the photographer. Without first-rate professional reproductions of my creations, there could be no book, nor one I was willing to attach my name to.

While we chatted between photo takes, I discovered that David had been commissioned as the photographer for a number of important exhibits and books. At the end of 2005, The Metropolitan Museum of Art in New York mounted a retrospective exhibition called RARA AVIS: Selections From The Iris Barrel Apfel Collection, and it was David who photographed every item for it. In 2002, he photographed the historical garments from Drexel University's Costume Collection, part of their Fashion Program, for their online museum. He was the sole photographer for two books by Bella Veksler, who taught Fashion Design and Fashion History at Drexel University, the Philadelphia Art Institute, and was Curator of the Drexel

University Historical Costume Collection. Published by Schiffer Publishing Ltd, the books are called *Lace: The Poetry of Fashion* (1998), and *The Fashionable Fan* (2000).

Reasonably sure I had found my photographer, his responses, once he saw the dolls, cinched it for me without hesitation, and without my having to see any of his work in advance of hiring him. He immediately saw the whimsy and the elegance, while commenting on the subtlest of details. He completely understood my work, and through multiple studio photo shoots, his enthusiasm and perfectionism never wavered. With each full shot and accompanying close-ups, he captured the colors and fine points of each art figure with pitch perfection, producing little works of art in themselves. I am immensely appreciative of his talent, skills, and professionalism, and can unequivocally say, this book would not be here for you to enjoy without David Gehosky's participation.

A Final Thought

I invite you, the reader, to share this journey into my world of whimsically elegant cats. Skillfully and elaborately costumed dolls are like theater performers. If they are good at their craft, the audience will accept what they want you to see, and want you to believe in. In short, IT IS ALL ABOUT THE PRESENTATION!

Aristocatic Gentleman

Height: 13"

The ARISTOCATIC GENTLEMAN represents the height of fashionable male attire at the onset of what is commonly referred to as the "Restoration Period." In 1660, upon his return from exile, Charles II restored the British monarchy, and brought with him this extreme fashion, which was popular in the French court. It lasted in England for roughly another decade. To our modern eye, it is difficult to comprehend how a gentleman could proudly appear in public wearing an ensemble so heavily festooned with such a overuse of lace and ribbons. The costumes featured silk or velvet ribbons, which had been formed into bunches and made up of countless loops, sometimes with as much as 250 yards of ribbon. They adorned every conceivable part of the suit, including shoulders, sleeves, waist, and knee-length pants, called "breeches." The latter were so wide they were named "petticoat breeches," suggesting a distinctly feminine aesthetic. Lace falls and ruffles descended from the "breeches," while bows and "rosettes" dotted many areas of the outfit. Even ringlets on the wig had bows! Plumes and ribbons were essential decorations on the brimmed hats.

The "doublet," or jacket, was purposely kept short so as to allow a white shirt of the finest cotton to peek out underneath, as well as below the elbow-length beribboned sleeves. Multiple buttons appeared on both the upper sleeves and jacket, which remained unbuttoned below the top one or two. In addition to the "jabot" and collar, beautiful laces edged the wide, gathered shirt's sleeves at the wrist, With the "periwig's" gradual increase in size, smaller collars replaced the elegant and distinctive wide "Cavalier collars," as they were now almost hidden by the masses of falling curls.

I used black silk brocade fabric for the ensemble, and edged the hems of both the jacket and skirt with beaded black braid. To replicate the abundance of ribbons, so critical to this fashion period, I used 7mm and 4mm wide black silk Japanese ribbon. These ribbons, readily available from doll costume suppliers, are especially soft, thereby permitting me to incorporate multiple bunched loops while staying true to the proportion of the doll. When translating fashion from life-size to a much smaller representation, it is imperative to keep scale in mind at all times through the careful use of fabric, trim, and accessories.

Although black was the preferred wig color, I chose gold curls to blend with the cat's complexion. Strategically placed splashes of red ribbons create a needed break of color. Black stockings accompanied black shoes with distinctive red heels and the requisite bow trim. The foppish mode is so over the top, as to appear more like a theater costume, feeling at once both amusing and ridiculous, yet, at the same time, fascinating in its exuberant detail.

I designed ARISTOCATIC GENTLEMAN to represent a faithful reproduction of the costume period discussed above, and all its basic elements are on display in our fashion template. Over and above the peacock quality of the costume, I aimed to make our ARISTOCAT, himself, appear a touch more comical but not cartoonish. To achieve this goal I gave him a shorter stature, which makes the foot/shoe size as well as the wig seem more outsized. It was fashionable during this period to strut about with a tall cane, here decorated with a bunched gold ribbon and a fish perched on top.

Standing squarely on both feet, showing off his outsized tail with ringed fingers, our ARISTOCATIC GENTLEMAN's delicately mustached face displays a look of utter, stoic boredom!

Autumn Splendor

Height: 18"

Women's fashion of the 1630s is well suited to represent the notion of abundance and bounty, which we associate with the Autumn Harvest season. The full-figured costume of the time is ideal for displaying not only the wondrous colors of nature, but also a wide assortment of embellishments ranging from man-made beads to tiny genuine acorns. Excellent resources for historical fashion particulars abound through paintings, especially those by Dutch artists. In England, Anthony Van Dyke was the court portrait painter of the British royal family, at the time, headed by Charles I, although this King eventually and literally lost his head to the executioner. Charles was married to the beautiful French-born Queen Henrietta Maria, who was a fashion setter of her time, and Van Dyke's portraits of her are nothing short of inspirational for costume aficionados.

HER ROYAL CATNESS, representing the costume period preceding AUTUMN SPLENDOR, features highly confining corsetry and an unnatural contraption, called the "farthingale." In comparing the two fashions silhouettes, SPLENDOR displays strikingly less constriction. As this new style evolves, the entire look moves from that of sharp severity to a sense of fullness and curves. For example, the pointed "stomacher," although still long, has a softer, rounded end, while a ribbon sash at what is now a higher waist, creates an interruption in the front length. By raising the waistline to just below the breasts, the bosom, in turn, appears more ample as does the whole upper body frame. Huge padded sleeves, formidable in size and construction, further exaggerate the shoulder breadth. Yet an additional layer of fabric, partially covering the upper sleeve, falls to mid-way, its two ends pulled and tied together with a bow or "rosette." The overall effect appears to gently divide the full sleeve into two massive puffs, the top half being larger than the bottom, in what is technically called a "Virago" sleeve.

The falling lace, or "Cavalier collar," style enhanced both feminine and masculine attire. Usually plain around the hem bottom, the abundant dress skirt fell attractively to the ground, and, as with this figure, sometimes opened to display a decorated "underskirt." To decorate the olive "dupioni" silk "underskirt," I used bronze colored metallic braid as well as an intricate beaded floral trim, which was originally a woman's neck choker. The weave and design of the synthetic dress fabric is a perfect choice as it contains autumnal colors in gentle swirls simulating falling leaves. Clusters of orange silk leaves and beads highlight the front edges of the full "overskirt."

Finally, I made the headdress to reflect the prevailing hairstyle. The coiffure at the time included a relatively flat top, bangs at the forehead, and ringlets standing slightly away from and to the side of the face. Remaining hair in back was pulled up into a topknot. In keeping with the doll's theme, her headdress consists of a riot of autumnal color and flourishes of leaves, acorns, beads, flowers, pods, and ribbons.

This lady is dedicated to one of my two dear daughters-in-law, Sarah, whose very favorite color is orange and, more importantly, is a phenomenally talented floral arranger with her own business. What better tribute to her than AUTUMN SPLENDOR, standing proud and tall, in just the right colors and representing nature's beauty?

Blue Rhapsody

Height: 18"

I have a confession to make. For most of my costume love life, I concentrated on historical fashion going back to the fifteenth century, but going forward until only the height of the romantic "Edwardian period," *c.*1905, with minor forays into pre-WWI. Perhaps I carried the sentimental notion that, with the onset of that horrendous war, the world had closed a chapter in history, never to appear again.

Then I discovered the utterly incredible work of "Erté." I am most taken with the costume period of roughly 1918 into the early 1920s, before the popular Flapper fashion took hold. There are a number of books written about this remarkable designer and his work, including one by this publisher. Other books offer compilations of numerous black and white illustrations, executed during the years of 1918-1932 for "Harper's Bazar," (spelled at the time with one a). They are among my most inspirational resources for this delicious fashion period, and, fortunately for all of us costume enthusiasts, Erté was a prolific illustrator. His "Art Deco" style was unique and, to many experts, transformational in the way he portrayed women. He presented his ladies as elongated, slim creatures, exquisitely clothed in languid softness, and with pronounced painted, facial features. Stance and posture can play an integral part in defining a fashion style. During RHAPSODY'S time, the "slouch" became the ideal, achieved by narrow hips thrown forward with accompanying flat bosom. The "slouch" gave the impression of an androgynous figure, and, although some contemporaries dismissed the look as distinctly unfeminine, I see it as both alluring and seductive.

Exemplifying the period, I posed the doll with the characteristic hand-on-hip, a look often seen in fashion illustrations of the time. The patterned deep blue-on-blue silk material of the coat has an unusually soft hand and lends itself to falling in gentle, asymmetric folds. Antique, pale blue fabric with a decidedly slinky feel, provides the requisite soft draping for the dress skirt. The warm orange color adds counterbalance to the cool blues. Given the broad variety of possible costume choices, I cherry-picked a combination of elements that work harmoniously together to produce a cohesive result. A number of fashion features contribute to the desired illusion of lanky height: a turban with upright feather, soft "dolman sleeves," tassels finishing off floor-trailing silk flaps or panels, uneven lengths of beads, a long gold chain, and high dramatic collar. Textural elements include blue silk fringing, white lace, "rosettes" of pale blue silk ribbon, and metallic braid of gold and blue. I constructed her hands from kid gloves and wired each finger, to enhance the delicate and flirtatious manner in which she holds the mirror. Heeled boots with white spat tops were common in footwear. Her long eyelashes, exaggerated facial makeup around the eyes, and prominent beauty mark derive directly from "Erté's" drawings. I suggest the reader refer to the doll, PINK PURRFECTION, for additional discussion points, applicable to this costume time. Every historical fashion period has its own unique and undeniable fascination, but this era now takes center stage in my lexicon. I could easily make a whole collection of figures just from this era.

I hope RHAPSODY would agree with my portrayal of her as confident in her beauty and choice of wardrobe, as she admires the finished outcome.

Cat in a Hat

Height: 11" total
8" seated figure

The wording of this title has several meanings. This little lady from mid-1890s is not only in a hat because she is wearing one, but also sitting inside one. I created the large hat for her as both a stage setting and a surface on which to display the many decorative millinery accents. Large bows, leaves, and silk flowers surround and fill the flat brim in conjunction with small hats, miniature birds, and nests.

At first glance, the 1890s costume style might resemble that of MISS KITTY, our exemplar of 1830s fashion. The comparison resides with the "leg-o-mutton" sleeve, the most noteworthy and pronounced dress feature in both. In order to give the illusion of an unusually tiny waist, the shoulders in each costume are disproportionately broad, thanks to the huge upper balloon shape of the sleeves, which then taper down narrowly to the wrists. Yet, the sleeves differ in their point of origin. They are lower down the arm in the earlier MISS KITTY, but at the higher shoulder seam in the later CAT IN A HAT. In the 1830s, large and fairly rigid panels, like large "epaulets," appeared at the juncture of the sleeve and armhole opening, whereas in the 1890s we see layers of frothy gathered lace. Apart from the characteristic "leg-of-mutton" sleeves, any similarity between the two fashions ends here.

Skirts were noticeably different. Wide, gathered, and often flounced in the 1830s, those of the 1890s were simpler in appearance. Cut in "gores," floor length, and designed to hug the hips, skirts gently flared out toward the hem in bell-like fashion. Jackets were similar to those of the preceding decade, displaying high necklines and collars, lapels, and lace "jabots." Tailoring for women had begun to come into its own, as ladies became interested in wearing suits and outfits for specific purposes, such as travel, employment, and sports. Although seated, the figure's very small waist size is evident. I refer the reader to a discussion of the hourglass figure associated with THE CAT'S MEOW, as it is equally pertinent to this fashion period.

Although bright saturated colors were often used during this period, I chose a more restrained palette so as not to interfere with the multi-faceted decor of the stage-set hat. I fashioned the jacket of greenish bronze silk with soft ecru antique laces, and "revers," or lapels, made of old patterned silk, trimmed with braid. Deep, dusty rose "velour," dotted with tiny beads, constitutes the skirt fabric, with coordinating rose silk for the sash and blouse. Her brooch, originally an earring, provides a touch of sparkle.

Our heroine, CAT IN A HAT, suggests a touch of mischievousness as she happily acts her part in a hat.

Cat's Cradle

Height: 15" total
13" seated figure

CAT'S CRADLE named after the finger held string game, is the only doll in the collection where the main character does not have a cat face. The head, part of a flea market doll, received an enhanced face with fake fur wig, eyebrows, and goatee. Peering over this genial character's shoulder, the baby cat in a silk knapsack is the feline in this instance. I fantasized this figure to be a jester employed by the court to entertain the royal prince. My photographer, David Gehosky's, own cat agreed, in a manner of speaking, to pose beautifully, but not before a great deal of coaxing and many bribes of treats.

The clothing presents many features of men's fashion from mid 1500s through *c.*1570s; however, the pointy shoes and large, soft turban-like hat are from an earlier period. In order to be historically accurate, many of the fashion features will be referred to by their technical names. The gentleman wears a jacket called a "doublet" with a short, gathered skirt. The skirt hangs over round-looking padded pants, called "trunk hose." Leg coverings consist of two distinct parts: On the upper leg are "canions," which are tubular in shape. They end below the knee, meeting the lower section of stockings, "nether-stocks," attached to the "canions" by a ribbon.

To elicit a light-hearted, comical look to this figure, I used a red/black/gold plaid "silk taffeta" for the "doublet" and heavier black silk with tiny white dots in the weave for the "trunk hose." Red and white with metallic gold silk brocade appears on the lower arms, the "canions," and the front chest. The hat and rumpled "nether-stocks," or stockings, are of gold "silk taffeta." Black and white striped silk form decorative cuffs covering his knobby knees. He wears a diagonal band embellished with gold, red, and light blue beaded embroidery, the latter matching the hat's plume as well as the beaded upholstered metal stool from which he nonchalantly dangles his long legs. I decorated the hat with braid, a plume, and my own gold pin with pearls. Despite differences in the various fabrics, they work well together from the standpoint of color, scale, and pattern.

THE BABY PRINCELING WATCHES THE STRING SKILLS OF OUR HUMOROUS HERO, CAT'S CRADLE, ECLIPSED ONLY BY A VERY DISINTERESTED LIVE CAT.

Catbird

Height: 18"

There really is such a thing as a catbird, a bird with a call like a meow. Given the awkward relationship between cats and birds, what better than to combine the two into one figure!

I drew on the historical period of mid-1780s to illustrate the CATBIRD concept, as the silhouette has an inherent bird-like quality. In fact, the puffed out chest, accentuated by a full "fichu" scarf is referred to as "pouter-pigeon," and the protruding back skirt, further accentuated by a padded "bum roll" under the skirt at the figure's lower back, suggests the bird's tail. The costume details spring from paintings and historical fashion plates of the time. Fashion plates, first appearing in the 1770s and often hand colored, were beautiful illustrations of contemporary and popular clothing styles. By the mid-nineteenth century, periodicals and journals made it possible to inform more and more women of the latest fashions. Almost a century later, fashion of the 1870s revisited a number of these previous style elements with the pigeon look and the introduction of a gentle "bustle." I could have selected this period instead, but chose not to for several reasons. The later 1870s fashion employed very intricate and complex draping of the "bustle" skirt. Rather, for this figure, I envisioned a simpler clothing style allowing for a full display of colorful, luxurious feathers on the skirt's train, the area I most associated with bird plumage. Consequently, I chose the 1780s style of "overdress," called "robe à l'anglaise" (English dress), which, while relatively uncomplicated in cut, is considerably enhanced by the "dupioni" silk's rich magenta color. Furthermore, I find the early French fashion depictions to exhibit a somewhat naughty quality to the ladies. Such a characteristic adds just the right touch of whimsical mischievousness to the notion of a bird and cat being integrally entwined and forced to coexist.

Dress skirts of the 1780s were ankle length and revealed the shoes, which I covered in silk fabric. I attached a wide, generously gathered "flounce" (or ruffle) at the hem of the striped silk "underskirt," as stripes were especially popular during the period. A side note about the striped fabric offers an example of using seemingly unmatched colors together. One of the stripes is actually a reddish color, but next to the strong magenta, the eye is fooled into seeing it as blending in with its more dominant neighbor. "Pinked" and gathered, the same stripe forms the trimming at the trained "overskirt's" front edges as well as on the three-quarter length sleeves. Soft old lace hangs gracefully below the cuffs. In silk fabrics white tends to be creamier, thereby mandating that laces be the same to maintain an aged look. Stark white would be out of place and stand out as brand new.

The use of such a hot and vibrant dress color calls for including complementary cool colors to provide resting places for the eye. Therefore, I employed sage green for the hand-embroidered vest/bodice, the shoes, and a spot in the hat, as well as a touch of blue at the neckline. Feathers, applied in abundant layers, represent the figure's bird quality and constitute a deliberate deviation from any literal rendering of the period. Yet, the all-important silhouette or outline of the costume, combined with the typical stance depicted in portraits and drawings of the time, are immediately recognizable and identifiable as that of the 1780s.

The hairstyle of countless curls standing wide out from the temples as well as flowing down the back, is typical of the period. Using several types of feathers, her lace-trimmed hat incorporates the important plumage motif.

I always knew she would hold a muff, therefore I created her stance to allow for the wide-spread elbows. To show off her dress to best advantage, it needs to be seen from a profile position, while her head is turned outward to be able to face the viewer with a touch of haughtiness. The bird peeking out of the muff adds a humorous note.

In short, this CATBIRD has no doubts whatsoever: She knows she looks fabulous!

Catch a Falling Star

Height: 16"

Leon Bakst (1866-1924) was a Russian painter, scene and costume designer. The most notable of costumers for the Ballet Russe, under the direction of Serge Diaghilev, after the turn of the twentieth century, Bakst revolutionized the depiction of sets and costume designs. His groundbreaking choices of sumptuous colors in unusual combinations were nothing short of extraordinary, and his creative embrace of eastern exotic influences makes his costumes supremely captivating.

As was the case with ORIENTAL PLUMAGE, I had practically no historical costume illustrations to refer to, and decided to present the costume as I imagined it. Picturing this figure dressed as a rajah prince, I turned to Bakst for my inspiration. I began by creating the gold silk turban, adorned with feathers and beads, held in place by a loose chinstrap composed of several rows of pearls. With upturned shoes and full pants below the coat completed, the exoticism of the outfit was firmly on its way, and I could turn to what I knew would be an embellisher's delight.

Fabrics of rich red, bronze/gold with accents of several blues, including light blue, navy, and turquoise, comprise the color palette. Four overlapping panels, two slightly longer red ones underneath, and two of bronze-colored fabric with a very tiny striped weave make up the coat's skirt. Each panel edge reveals an embroidered ribbon trim, all, in turn, decorated with various types of adornment. Colorful, woven ribbon appears as a cuff of the upper, puffed sleeve and repeats as a border all around the bolero-style jacket. To make all the lace trims look gilded, I used a gold paint pen to give an old antique appearance to what were originally white laces. I created dangling beads at the hem, thereby adding a playful fringe to what is otherwise a fairly tailored coat.

The silver and gold stars started out as buttons and costume jewelry components. Extremely tiny stars dot the red under-sleeves, turban and, finally, the blue velvet base.

The song tells us: "Catch a falling star and put it in your pocket – Never let it fade away." With our prince's basket of precious treasures securely in one hand, and seeing the loving gaze he bestows on his newly caught star in the other, we can be assured that CATCH A FALLING STAR, for one, will never let it fade away.

Chatelaine, the Cat-Can Dancer

Height: 7"

The idea for CHATELAINE came from the French can-can dancers of the 1890s, and whose depiction is popularly associated with the paintings of French artist Toulouse-Lautrec. I created this porcelain lady in slightly taller than dollhouse scale and selected her name to inject a touch of whimsy. Chat means cat in French.

Bright orange curly hair enhances her saucy presentation, while the orange silk of her wide skirt carries through the vibrant color. Edged at the hem with a border of small feathers, the skirt reveals many layers of lace ruffles on the very important "petticoat" underneath, which her raised knee coquettishly displays to great advantage. Black leather boots reflect typical footwear of the time. Her large sleeves, of dusty green "silk taffeta," are suggestive of the "leg-of-mutton" style of the 1890s decade, and a draped panel of plaid silk around the hips continues down the skirt with two long sashes. The color, black, gives definition to the edging of the sash panels through the use of black fringe and "picot" trim.

I think it safe to say that, with her leg ready to kick up and out, and her unmistakably exuberant face and body expression, CHATELAINE has secured a safe place in the annals of CAT-CAN dancing!

Clowning Around

Height: 27" total
22" seated figure

Several years ago I bought this whimsical goose with the long, spindly legs, although at the time I had nothing definite in mind as to how I would use it. Since then it has lived among my collection of potential props until just the right inspiration struck me in the form of CLOWNING AROUND. Blue flocking with sprinkles of cheap glitter covered the bird's body, which I covered over with a fresh new coat of soft white loopy fake fur. I added knobby knees to give more definition to the legs and covered them with gold "lamé" stockings atop the gilded boots. A small crown sits on the white fluff of hair, and a full tail of marabou feathers adds a lavish flourish to the figure.

Having no preconceived fashion period in mind when I began the clown, I proceeded with pure fantasy. Inspired by the paisley cotton overskirt of blues and pinks, I assembled a collection of five different cotton prints in addition to two solid blue silks and deep blue silk ribbon bows. Several layers of generously ruffled fabric appear at the legs and shoulders, the latter covered by panels, loosely reminiscent of "epaulets." I used a variety of trims, including beading, ruched ribbons, "yo-yo circles" of the same print fabrics as the ensemble, and white laces. Atop the wig of multi-colored knitting wool, I placed a tall, fez-shaped headdress with pink plumes. The hat's oversized piece of costume jewelry with dangling beads adds unexpected drama.

Although the conceptual framework of the costume is not from a specific period, certain elements echo the past, most notably the British "Restoration" (from 1660) in the beribboned "overskirt" and bloomer pants. The shoulders hint at the "Renaissance."

I painted the delicate mask directly onto the face and especially wanted the doll to be graceful and lithe. Pensively gazing at a ball attached to several gold hoops and balanced astride the now transformed bird, sits a very elegant clown, CLOWNING AROUND.

Floral Exuberance

Height: 19"

This doll reflects the fashion of *c.* 1818 during what we refer to as the Empire period in France, and the Regency in England. Extending from 1811 to 1820, Regency owes its name to the rule of the British King George IV. He ruled as proxy, i.e., Prince Regent, (hence the name Regency) for his father, King George III, of American Revolution fame, when the latter was judged unfit to rule. When George III died in 1820, George IV continued to reign, but now as King in his own right.

I was well familiar with the era's silhouette and the prominent fashion features, reflected in large bonnets and slim dresses with extremely high waists. Upon reviewing costume history of the period, I was surprised to learn how much decoration already appeared at skirt hems between 1815 and 1820. Borders of fairly simple ribbon or lace bands edged skirt only a few years earlier, but by 1815, fashion drawings show an array of deep, three-dimensional puffs of ribbons, "rosettes," frills, and flowers. FLORAL's silhouette is unmistakably of the period, and I felt comfortable employing the wide assortment of flowers I had planned on using, without deviating too far from the essence of the fashion.

By exaggerating the length of the doll's body below the waist, I am drawing in the viewer to focus on the skirt with its highly adorned hem and vertical panels. For the dress, I used a light silk in white, as this was one of the most frequently used colors at the time. Two rows of gathered, antique lace provide gentle texture at the bottom of the skirt, while an abundance of silk flowers in peach, dark mauve, and deep red festoons the area immediately above.

FLORAL wears a purplish/mauve "dupioni" silk "pelisse," a coat-like overdress worn anywhere from three-quarters to full length. Descending from the belted high waist, I created a series of six panels: Three are triangular *V*s, and three are soft, puffy panels of decorated lavender "silk taffeta." Flowers, some edged with gold paint, boldly surround the front panel, while bright green leaves and curled ribbon accent the ensemble with more color. Around her neck, the doll displays several rows of peach flowers, sprinkled with tiny crystals, meant to simulate a form of "ruff," called a "betsie." The term derives from the name of Elizabeth I, as it refers to the lace "ruffs" worn during the "Elizabethan Era."

Hair of the time was drawn up in the back to form a small top-knot while tight curls framed the upper part of the face. Tiny flowers in colors of mauve and lavender, in conjunction with purple ribbons, formed as ringlets, simulate hair curls. Bonnets came into their own during this time, and, although shapes and sizes may have changed, they remained popular and an essential part of feminine attire for most of the nineteenth century. The wide brim of this large, pale yellow silk bonnet charmingly surrounds her face, while flowers, fringing, and feathers embellish the hat's tall crown. In one leather-gloved hand, she fingers the bonnet ties, while a lavender "tulle" shawl casually dangles from the other.

FLORAL MAY EXHIBIT EXUBERANCE IN HER DRESS, BUT SHE, HERSELF, WITH LONG-LASHES AND DOWNCAST EYES IS THE EMBODIMENT OF DELICATE MODESTY AND DEMUR GRACE, QUALITIES SO ADMIRED IN LADIES OF THE TIME.

Her Royal Catness

Height: 18"

In the process of designing and developing HER ROYAL CATNESS, I found myself creating a mini story about her leading, in turn, to the addition of the long-suffering dog. He is the official Royal Tail Carrier, who inherited the prestigious position from his father, a post passed down through the male, ancestral line. His unusual costume contains surviving elements from earlier time periods, and explains the discrepancy between his outfit and that of the mistress he serves. Her Highness wears the British court fashion of *c.*1615, during the reign of James I, who succeeded Queen Elizabeth I on the English throne. In a twist of historical irony, James was the son of Mary Stuart, i.e. Mary, Queen of Scots, the very Queen referred to in MARY, MARY, QUITE CATRARY, whose execution was ordered by Elizabeth.

Drawn from historical portraits and illustrations of the time, this doll's dress is an accurate representation of the period's fashion. The gown's ankle-length skirt commands the viewer's attention as it falls in a great many folds from the "farthingale," an impressive horizontal drum-shaped structure generally associated with Elizabethan fashion. After the death of Elizabeth in 1603, Anne of Denmark, wife of King James I, continued to wear the "farthingale," and it remained in fashion until she died in 1619. Other costume features continued into James' reign: a low, narrow waist combined with the long, slim, and rigid triangular-shaped panel, called a "stomacher," plus a wide circular ruffle around the waist. A lace "whisk" collar, designed to stand high at the back of the head, was particularly popular. Long tight sleeves, ending in lace cuffs, acquired added dimension from "hanging sleeves." These were strips of dress material that fell down the back from the shoulders, and appear to have had little function other than to offer another layer of decoration.

A seemingly limitless profusion of surface ornamentation adorned the most splendid and costly materials. I found a fabric with simulated gold threads woven throughout for the dress, and, although not particularly expensive yardage, it gives an appropriately rich appearance. I constructed the "hanging sleeves" and luxurious "underskirt" from a rare piece of antique silk brocade, the latter highlighted with randomly placed crystal beads. As floral motifs were especially popular, I incorporated them wherever possible in our lady's lavishly adorned royal gown. The brocade fabric's purple and rose shades dictate the primary accent colors for the beaded flowers throughout the garment. Prominently incorporated on the "stomacher" design, they give the impression of encrusted gems. Pearls, widely used during the previous century, continued to be very much in vogue, and I incorporated them in a rope necklace and in the multiple rows of her choker. Above a single row of pearls at the hem edge of the "overskirt," I embroidered a series of pearl flowers. Additional pearl designs appear on both the "underskirt" and the rich borders of the "overskirt." In order to simulate vines, leaves and flowers on the dress borders, I appliquéd sections of faux-gilded lace, snipped out from a larger piece.

Accessories include a fur trimmed gold fan in one hand while a hanging "pomander," or perfume receptacle, attached to a long chain from the waist, dangles from the other hand.

HER CATNESS is clearly of royalty as her proud bearing and crown attest. I would, however, be remiss if I did not point out the family crest appliquéd on the dog's cape: namely, the royal cat paw.

Coming full circle back to my imaginary story, the most fitting subtitle is: Some are born to rule, others to serve!

I **AM** *trying to look regal!*
I am **TRYING** *to look regal!*
I am trying to look **REGAL!**

Height: 16"

The inspiration for this theme came from one of my cats, Algernon, who, unfortunately, is no longer with us. A black and gray tabby with beautiful markings, he had a way of half-closing one eye while sitting upright in deep thought. One felt as if he could not quite decide which image of his multi-faceted personality to convey to us mere humans, who lovingly watched him with curiosity. Regardless of which one of the title's three parts the reader thinks best personifies this doll, there can be little doubt that His Majesty is having a really hard time!

This fashion style of *c.* 1670 immediately followed in time that of ARISTOCATIC GENTLEMAN. With a diminution of the previous decade's excesses, the male attire that emerged represented the transformation of men's clothing. The new emphasis on coats and vests or waistcoats set the stage for the evolution of what we now recognize as the modern three-piece suit: trousers, vest, and jacket. His Highness models a knee-length silk waistcoat with gold heraldic design and brushed gold bead buttons down the front. His coat, of similar length to the long vest, is worn open while bunches of ribbons adorn the elbow-length sleeves. I lavishly applied rich gold braiding as trim to the coat and the flowing mantle. Working in concert with the more traditional reds and gold of royalty, the introduction of strong, deep turquoise offers unexpected vibrancy and elegant punch. I used turquoise not only for the knee-length pants peeking out under the waistcoat, but also for the sash, and the crown. The color repeats in beaded detail on the elegant trim, visible on the cape or mantle's turned back edges. Numerous gold beads, matching those on the vest, dot the cape, and white fake fur edges its collar. A gold lion, symbol for head-of-state, hangs from the fringed and beaded sash around his waist.

He sports a voluminous "periwig" in popular black hair color, but his face appears worried and unsure. One chubby hand holds a gold scepter, while the other desperately tries to keep his outsized crown from falling off his head. Brocade fabric shoes look uncertain on legs turned inwards as he tries to maintain his balance and steady his pose.

EACH OF THE TITLE'S THREE CONCEPTS SUGGESTS A DIFFERENT EMPHASIS, BUT I FEEL THEY ALL FUNCTION TOGETHER – WHAT ABOUT YOU?

If You Want the Best Seat in the House, You'll Have to Move the Cat!

Height: 12" seated figure

This cheeky fellow is not about to budge from his favorite chair. His whole body language suggests he is here to stay until he is ready to move on. I took my influence for this doll from a portrait of Richard Sackville, the 3rd Earl of Dorset, painted in 1613 by Wm. Larkin.

The doll's long shapely legs display black stockings, made of cut-up pantyhose, while his leather shoes are adorned with outsized gold "rosettes." I constructed his full, puffed "breeches" out of a colorful, knit material with tight pleats, which came from a woman's blouse I found at a thrift shop. The fabric colors, which determined the rest of the costume's palette, repeat in the jewel tones of his turquoise "doublet" or jacket and his magenta silk cloak.

Using my favorite technique of gilding white or ecru lace, I placed pieces, cut out from a larger piece onto the front and sleeves in a deliberate pattern so as to give the impression of rich brocade. For sparkle, I added pale turquoise rhinestones to the front of the closed jacket, while long lace cuffs and "epaulets" finish, respectively, the sleeve wrists and shoulders. This "doublet" style displays decorated, overlapping tabs at the bottom, a design feature common during the time. Narrow metallic gold, or "lamé" ribbon acts as an outline on all the jacket details. The silk ribbon bows, appearing at the points where the tabs join the jacket hem, are not only decorative, but serve a function. They represent the ends of ties that attach the stockings to the "doublet." This is accomplished by threading ribbons through a series of holes in the garment above the tabs. Despite the increasing popularity of large "whisk" collars, this fellow is hesitant to give up his beloved "ruff," as he likes the way it frames his face. As men, at this time, wore cloaks inside as well as outdoors, our gentleman keeps his on and loosely tied across his chest. More faux gold, simulating embroidery, decorates the turned back cloak edges.

Although hair ringlets were more common in subsequent years, and had only begun to make an appearance at the time of this fashion, I felt the need to give him these artfully placed curls as well as a goatee and thin mustache. Finally, a lace-edged handkerchief hangs delicately from his jeweled fingers. Rings were particularly popular for men, especially those worn on the thumb.

Clearly of privilege and aristocracy, he knows he looks every bit the fashionably dressed gentleman, not to mention beguilingly handsome.

Lady Gwendolyn

Height: 19"

In 2010, I went to the fabulous Neue Galerie in New York for an exhibit, called Postcards of the Wiener Werkstätte (Vienna Workshop). Although the display covered a wide selection of subject matter, it should come as no surprise that I was immediately struck, if not smitten, by those depicting fashion from 1911-1912. Of the many talented artists who produced for the Workshop, the work of Mela (Melanie) Koeler particularly affected me. A prolific graphic designer, she produced a rich pictorial collection of women in the prevailing fashion of those years. LADY GWENDOLYN, who, incidentally, I named after my cat, is the three-dimensional embodiment of those lovely illustrations.

During the pre-World War I years, following the "Edwardian" period's fussy, frilly clothing, women's fashion went through enormous changes. Waistlines rose in pseudo Grecian or Empire style, while skirts became shorter – just enough to expose the shoe toe. The new skirt became so narrow that ladies could only walk with tiny steps, resulting in what became known as the "hobble skirt." In order to maintain the sought-after slender, tubular style yet permit normal walking, slits in the front or side skirt were essential. The "peg-top skirt" was another popular style, where more fullness appeared at the hips, but the skirt still fell to absurdly narrow hem widths. Paul Poiret, an important French fashion designer with a strong flair for the theatrical, was a major influence, not only in the introduction of a high waist, but also of the dramatic overskirt, called the "minaret tunic." Sometimes referred to as the "lampshade tunic," and paired with the "hobble or peg-top skirt," it was designed to flare out and away from the body, often with the aid of wire at the hem edge. This doll wears such a skirt, with stiff braid at the hem to give it the requisite flared appearance.

Although open necklines became popular, I chose to make a high collar for the sake of proportion and equalizing what are essentially four divisions in this doll: straw hat, upper body, muff, and lower body.

Extremely large hats from the previous decade continued in fashion with no diminution in the astonishing display of lavish trims, bows, flowers, and especially feathers, much to the great alarm of bird lovers. LADY GWENDOLYN reflects the silhouette and all the costume features that immediately identify and date the outfit to *c.* 1912. The oversize muff, was the overriding inspiration for the doll. I wanted the muff to be nothing short of impressive, commanding attention as the primary focal point. Fully adorned with fringe, laces, and a large silk ribbon bow, I applied richly colored teal silk flowers to create the lush floral composition, while in the center, I placed an heirloom pendant from my mother.

The color palette of this doll came together only after I had planned a different combination, but the end result is truly striking, far exceeding my own expectations. The discussion that follows is one example of how the creative process may proceed and lead to delicious surprises. When I began this doll, I knew the salmon silk "charmeuse," a soft fabric with a slinky quality, would be an important component, and originally planned on deep gray silk for the contrasting color. After much attention to purchasing the appropriate color embellishments, I started work. Salmon and gray work extremely well together, yet, as I continued, I instinctively felt something was not right. The colors, although beautiful, were not dramatic or strong enough for the end result I had in mind. By keeping the salmon as a constant, I experimented with other possible contrast colors, such as greens, blues, black, and browns. A piece of chocolate brown silk jumped out of the pack, and I had a eureka moment when I realized it was the right color... but the wrong fabric. The answer called for a totally different surface texture: velvet. Modern velvets are usually too thick and heavy to use on a small figure, but "velour," made with lycra, gives the same appearance as velvets. Both soft and malleable, "velour" comes in a wonderful range of colors, readily available in higher end fabric stores. Fortunately, I live relatively near New York, and can troll the fabric district's material and trim stores in person. For those not so fortunate, most of the shops have Internet sites for shopping.

Shifting color gears, I purchased anew, and with the addition of the teal color in the flowers, LADY GWENDOLYN emerged most satisfactorily. I present this account to illustrate how essential it is to heed one's inner creative voice, even though it may result in inconvenience.

I CAN ONLY HOPE THAT MY REAL LADY GWENDOLYN IS AS PROUD OF HER NAMESAKE AS I AM.

A Lady of Quality

Height: 17"

A LADY OF QUALITY refers to a woman of high social standing and fine character. Exemplified by the figure presented here, this fetching damsel charmingly raises her lush white beribboned tail in a hand covered with black leather mittens. Her downcast eyes, rimmed by long lashes, coupled with just the right head tilt, emphasize a demure quality and social grace.

Creating a fashion ensemble with only one or two colors presents an interesting challenge. By removing the option of multiple colors, the designer needs, instead, to create visual interest and stimulation through appropriate selection of fabrics and trims; that is, the right variety of like-colored pattern, weave, and texture. The various designs and materials need to work together in harmony, proportion, and scale. I settled on a black and white combination, and quickly discovered how many permutations of basic black and basic white exist. For added visual excitement, I strategically punctuated the ensemble with red. I used eight different black/white fabrics and trims, including stripes, in some cases cut on the bias, plus checks, flowers, and brocade.

The elegant lady before us wears fashion of the late seventeenth century, from *c.*1685 through the end of the decade. Women of this period went to great lengths, literally, to give the impression of height. The high headdress, called "fontange," was constructed of laces, ribbons and "lappets" which fell over the shoulders and/or down the back. Of varying heights, the most extreme of these head adornments, which were worn at a slight forward tilt off the forehead and often referred to as towers, became so unwieldy that women eventually abandoned them. I chose to give my figure a modest "fontange," in a fan-shaped affair. Copious loops of soft silk ribbon simulate the characteristic high curled hairstyle of the day. Near the elbow, sleeves terminate in cuffs of black fake fur, while soft puffs of lace-edged fine cotton show below. Through tight corsetry, several features contribute to create the sought-after vertical line; namely, the fitted bodice, small waist, and long pointy front bodice panel, called a "stomacher."

The skirt, generally referred to as an "underskirt," to distinguish it from the one worn on top, was heavily decorated with numerous trim variations. Despite its placement as an "underskirt," it was, nevertheless, the more important of the two skirts from the perspective of embellishment. Gathered to the waist, it fell in generous folds to the ground. The trained "overskirt" pulled away from the garment's front at the hips, folding around to the back where the edges came together.

Many fashion pictures of the time depict what appear to be horizontal stripes on the underskirt. Rather than, literally, apply lines of trim directly onto a single skirt fabric, I created the illusion of horizontality by forming three separate skirt tiers. Although each tier is distinctly unlike the other, it is through the deliberate repetition of three of the fabrics in different combinations and their coordination with appropriate trims, that the illusion of stripes evolves. Adornments include beading, ribbons, and fringing, which was much in vogue. The "overskirt," trimmed with black lace, repeats some of the same fabrics, while "rosettes" are made of tiny black and white check ribbon. Pearls accentuate the brocade stomacher.

THE SILHOUETTE AND OVERALL IMPRESSION OF THIS DRESS STYLE ARE BOTH FLATTERING AND GRACIOUSLY ELEGANT. THERE CAN BE NO DOUBT THAT WE SEE BEFORE US A LADY OF FINE BREEDING AND, INDEED, OF THE HIGHEST QUALITY.

Mary, Mary, Quite Catrary

Height: 16"

There is hardly a nursery rhyme book that does not include *Mary, Mary, Quite Contrary*. Although the verse's origins are unclear, I prefer the popular theory that suggests it refers to Mary Stuart, more commonly referred to as Mary, Queen of Scots. Sadly, she came to a tragic end in her failed attempts to unseat Queen Elizabeth I from the British throne. This Mary should not be confused with the British queen, known as "Bloody Mary," the daughter of Henry VIII and Catherine of Aragon.

As the historical Scottish Queen Mary lived during the "Tudor" era of the mid-1500s, I present this Mary in the fashion of that time. Her silhouette displays all the essential features of the period, the distinct manner in which the clothes fit the body, and a strikingly stiff stance. Portraits of the time almost invariably showed ladies with elbows angled out and away from the body and hands held together over the lower mid-section, a position which may have been dictated by cumbersome sleeve construction. The distinctive and recognizable arm covering consisted of three main components: upper arm, false sleeve and outer sleeve. Whereas the upper sleeve was very tight, the lower half consisted of padded and stiffened false sleeves from elbow to wrist. These false sleeves provided a perfect surface for elaborate and gorgeously intricate designs. The curved section of the false sleeve edge revealed small puffs of the chemise undergarment on display at strategic intervals. Comprising the third component was the outer sleeve, which, when turned back, gave the appearance of a very long, deep cuff. The wrist ruffles were art works in themselves, ranging from fine lace to extraordinary embroidery, and/or jeweled accents. The gown gave the illusion of two triangles. The inverted upper triangle owed its shape to a hinged, padded iron corset, designed to flatten the chest into an unyielding bodice, thereby contributing to the typical upright, rigid posture, while probably causing considerable discomfort. At the cone-shaped bottom section, a gathered overskirt flared away in triangular formation revealing a flat "underskirt." A padded "hip roll," hidden under the skirt folds at the base of the bodice, created a gently rounded appearance, especially towards the dress back, and from there, the skirts continued to fall gently to the ground. The doll's high gold braid at her neck suggests a small "ruff."

The "French hood" is the headpiece we typically associate with the "Tudor" fashion. It consisted of essentially two parts: the hood containing the hair in back, while the crescent shape, often bejeweled, framed the face.

Despite the profusion of rich trims, embroideries and the use of fine jewels, this was an especially severe fashion, made more somber by the use of heavy fabrics often in dark colors. My choice of silk fabrics, both lighter in color and weight, presents an airy backdrop for a garden in full bloom. Flowers on the headdress and sleeves, as well as the use of leaf-like ribbon trim to edge the "overskirt," complement the dress focus: i.e., the elaborate "underskirt." The exposed yellow silk triangle presents a perfect blank canvas upon which to create a garden filled with hand embroidered and appliquéd flowers, silk leaves, and beads. I selected reds, strong pinks, oranges, and purples of differing intensities to accentuate buds and blossoms. They are critical to injecting the wow factor, and make the eye go straight to the main stage. Tiny real shells finish off the hem while silver bells dangle from her hands. The use of a cool blue color on the hanging sleeve cuffs offsets the warm colors of the dress. I did not include the maids from the rhyme, as they seemed superfluous. This doll represents a good example of how to take a specific historical fashion and move away from a literal rendition to an artistic translation, while still maintaining its fundamental characteristics.

MARY, MARY, QUITE CATRARY STANDS PROUDLY BEFORE HER AUDIENCE, READY TO HAVE HER PORTRAIT PAINTED.

Mary, Mary, Quite Contrary,
How does your garden grow?
With cockle shells and silver bells
And little maids all in a row.

Miss Kitty Tended to Overdress for Everything

Height: 18"

Dressed in "dernier cri" fashion, constructed of fine silks and laces, this lady carries a rag-filled pail and mop to face her housework! In order to illustrate the title of this doll, I required a fashion period that conveyed a sense of the absurd. I needed look no further than the mid-1830s.

The silhouette of that time offers an excellent example of the lengths to which fashion could go in order to achieve a sought-after look. In this instance, the goal was to demonstrate an exceptionally tiny waist, achieved by the obligatory tight corset, and by employing a deft form of illusion. By extending the width of the skirt, while simultaneously making the sleeves as broad as possible, the waist appeared ever smaller. Tightly gathered at the waistline, the skirt gradually flared out and away from the body toward the hemline, thanks to several starched "petticoats." In order to hold and maintain the enormous shape of the sleeves, the wearer required artificial extenders, including baskets, pillows, or whalebone often tied onto the upper arms. The breadth of the upper body seemed even wider through the addition of large panels on top of the sleeves, and giving the impression of exaggerated "epaulets." The resulting outline consisted of a huge upper sleeve affair beginning slightly below the shoulder and abruptly tapering to a tightly cuffed wrist. Known as "leg-of-mutton" sleeves, owing to their shape, they required a surprisingly large amount of fabric to achieve the desired result.

The distinctive coiffure adds to this peculiar fashion silhouette with a profusion of tight curls elaborately framing the upper half of the face. What became known as the "Apollo knot," particularly for evening attire, involved braided and/or looped artificial hair, adorned with a wide variety of trimmings.

Daytime head covering for indoors took on an asymmetrical hat-like quality with layers of gathered lace, interspersed with ribbons, bows, flowers and feathers. My homemaker, as it were, wears just such a confection. I deliberately took the fashion to an extreme through the use of ostentatiously colorful trims placed within the folds of antique laces and finished off the indoor hat with a big silk bow tied under and to the side of her chin. I needed the composition of the hat to play an important part in conveying the humor that is part and parcel of this doll. The purple ribbons and rosettes, silk sash, flowers, and bead trim of a lush shade of fuschia along with bits of deep teal were taken directly from the palette of rich colors in the silk taffeta skirt and "epaulets." Such strong hues require equally saturated color for the bodice; in this case, a bright yellow silk. Fan-like placement of matching yellow braid on the bodice front contributes to the illusion of a narrow waistline.

Yellow strips of bias-cut piping, placed both vertically and horizontally on the skirt, provide what I feel is a needed interruption in the bold plaid, lest it appear blocky. White laces and a finely embroidered white apron add a measure of cool elegance.

FOR MISS KITTY, NO MATTER THE JOB AT HAND AND REGARDLESS OF WHAT OTHERS MAY THINK, IT IS ALL ABOUT MAKING THE RIGHT PRESENTATION!

Moon Queen

Height: 19"

I begin this discussion by recommending that the reader turn to the descriptions of two other dolls appearing in this book, BLUE RHAPSODY and PINK PURRFECTION. They cover some of the same pre-1920s fashion elements I took into consideration when creating MOON QUEEN. Despite certain commonalities in the overall silhouette, this moon devotee's ensemble represents a much looser translation of the period, and is, by far, the most theatrical. Even the body stance, while acknowledging her audience, suggests she is on stage.

It is the evening sky that enables us to see the moon in all its glistening beauty; consequently, the colors of night determine this doll's dramatic costume. The springboard for the ensemble was a wide ribbon of gauzy navy blue interwoven with bright silver embroidery. I selected a deep blue silk "charmeuse" for the "overdress," and a gray/silver knit material, covered with sparkling silver for the "underskirt" and lower sleeves. Rich burgundy with metallic threads make up the accent color of both skirt panels and front bodice. The choice of stark white for her headdress, shoulder petals and face color, creates an essential contrast.

Despite the extravagance of the ensemble, I wanted to maintain the effect of a lean, elegant line, so typical of post-WWI fashion. Wherever possible, therefore, I incorporated verticality to encourage the viewer to look down and up the figure. My ample use of beading served two purposes. They introduce both restrained shine, while also affording an opportunity to create the kind of artistic interest that ribbon alone does not always achieve. Silver crescent moons, dangling from threaded bead lengths of dark mauve and clear crystal beads, hang gracefully down the front in uneven lengths. Hemmed with a narrow edging of gray fake fur, the soft fabric of the "underdress" falls gently to the ground and puddles around her feet. Two trailing burgundy panels, one along each dress side, are outlined in silver metallic braid. Clear and blue beads at the ends give an impression of fringe, while several lengths of blue beads decorate the white tail. I arranged the inspirational blue and silver ribbon into a series of multiple loops, and placed delicate, long silver tassels at the ends. To offset the raised waist, I introduced a modified "stomacher," using a thin strip of the burgundy for color interest.

The headdress is a fantasy combination of various feathers, while pearls on clear nylon wire seem suspended in air. I adapted the loose chains under her chin and the circlet of rhinestones above her eyes from "Erté" fashion illustrations. Lighter blue silk ribbon cascades gently, ending with a long earring for embellishment. The same ribbon is wrapped softly in such a way as to give the impression of a high neck.

Gracefully dangling a crescent and a sparkling star in each hand, MOON QUEEN displays her royal status with a lunar crown and silver, facial beauty spot in the shape of a partial moon. With every reason to be a proud embodiment of the night sky, she appears before us dusted in sparkles of moon dust.

Oriental Plumage

Height: 15"

As I ventured into the costume world of another culture and continent, this figure presented a distinct challenge. Unlike the easier accessibility of Japanese fashion literature, it is difficult to find complete color examples of royal historic Chinese costume. Having to confine myself to bits and pieces of illustration and description, I settled on conveying the impression of a Chinese Imperial lady. The two most important elements for me were the dress and most especially the headdress.

Once I had painted the appropriate facial features, I tackled the headdress, employing as a foundation a scrap of antique upholstery fabric. New heavier lace, which I aged with antique gold paint, comprises the ornate edging designed to give the impression of gold metal work. Beads and costume jewelry simulate jewels including those placed within the spaces of the headdress edging. New "findings," chosen for their old-world qualities add finishing touches throughout the presentation.

In searching for just the right textiles to convey one's inspiration, consider going beyond what we think of as traditional fabric sources. In this case, the tangerine and black brocade of the gown looks like silk, but is of soft synthetic material, originally part of a new decorative pillow. Here also is an example of a larger pattern, nevertheless, working on a much smaller scale figure. Various ribbons, selected for color and design, comprise the trims. A tiny bit of bright magenta at the neckline adds an unexpected spot of visual punch, while the cool turquoise color here and there keeps the richness of the outfit from overwhelming the eye.

The PLUMAGE in the title derives from her pet bird that this princess lovingly admires on her finger. Chinese royalty sported long, red fingernails, with special emphasis on the extra long gold-filigreed index finger.

The birdhouse started out as a Christmas ornament, which I recovered with a Chinese embroidered silk scarf. The stand began life as a tea-light holder, which I gilded and adorned with climbing gold wire and pearls.

DESPITE THE COSTUME'S OPULENT QUALITY, ORIENTAL PLUMAGE PRESENTS AN AURA OF SWEET DELICACY.

Pink Purrfection

Height:18"

Some of the best ideas often present themselves when you have not planned for them. As anyone with a passion for fabrics knows, to literally feel and play around with materials is perfectly normal behavior, even in public! During one of my very frequent trips to the neighborhood Jo-Ann Fabric and Crafts mega store on an unrelated project, I happened upon a spring collection of lovely pink cottons. I quickly became taken with the many possibilities of working with one color, and began to pull together a combination of three distinctively different designs all in pinks: a solid with random tufts of the same color, an all-over floral, and a stripe. With these choices in hand, I set out to find the oh-so-important trims and embellishments. The selection of warm taupe for a much-needed contrasting trim came as a delightful and unexpected surprise, but only after much experimentation with color options. Having added a few deeper shades of pink netting and fringe, the gentle taupe afforded me the perfect color accent to keep the ensemble visually in balance.

The edge of the long jacket gives the impression of intricately embroidered needlework. I achieved the look by using contemporary "venise" lace, which sells by the yard. It was, however, extremely wide: the right color, but clearly the wrong scale. By strategically cutting it apart and reducing its size to meet my needs, I was able to custom design my own decoration. The leaves came from a different trim, and the thread-covered balls come attached to a ribbon strip. I used a length of pink boa for the tail as well as the unusual hair/hat confection. I hand-ruffled silk ribbon for the collar and topped off her head decor with a crown, which has no special significance in this case, except for the fact that I love crowns. The use of deep wine for the furled parasol adds an exclamation point of color.

I refer the reader to the discussion of BLUE RHAPSODY as this doll has similar features. Both display stances suggesting the "slouch" posture on a willowy frame: The clothing makes no attempt to call attention to natural curves of a female body. Although each wears a vest or waistcoat, the coat-like jacket of PURRFECT differs as it brings to mind a style of overcoat worn by men a century earlier. Nevertheless, the figure appears unmistakably feminine. Drawing my inspiration from the same era as RHAPSODY, that of *c.*1920, I looked not only to "Erté" but also to costumes created by his contemporaries for the theater and dance halls. Consequently, this figure is more theatrical, with exaggerated cuffs, frothy wrist gathers, and marabou fur hair.

Although the skirt styles are very different, both are authentic to the time, for there were all manner of variations, including, and perhaps especially, in lengths. This brings up the vexing problem of hemlines in the post-war years just before and after 1920. I have read numerous discussions by fashion authorities, and what emerges is a confusing picture of what some have called elusive hemlines. Skirt lengths went up and down repeatedly, fluctuating between below the knees, ankle length and mid-calf. Often the lengths were different in the very same garment, created by panels of uneven lengths. People tend to associate the whole 1920s decade with the short-skirted Flapper fashion. In actuality, early Flapper dresses were generally mid-calf and the shorter length did not take hold in a big way until the end of the '20s. By the onset of the 1930s, hems were on their way back down again. This discussion would not be complete without making mention of changeable waistlines. Before 1920, waists were higher, dropping to their natural line with the approach of the new decade, and then falling further to the hips by the mid '20s, finally returning back to normal in the '30s.

I THINK IT IS SAFE TO SAY THAT UPON ENTERING A CROWDED ROOM, ALL EYES WOULD TURN TO THIS FASHION DIVA AND HEADS WOULD NOD WITH APPROVAL AT HER UTTER PURRFECTION.

Pretty in Paper

Height: 14"

This petite miss is eager to share a secret: her entire ensemble is made of paper! In an effort to expand my dollmaking skills, I wanted to create a figure using completely different materials. The idea occurred to me that instead of fabric materials, laces, silk florals and cloth trims, I would use only paper or anything non-fabric. Through periodic experimentation with decoupage and collage over the years, I had familiarized myself with different types of papers, and their individual characteristics, but never worked with them as one would with textiles.

I know nothing about paper other than my experience with decorator and fine art papers, available at specialty art supply shops, and which seem to contain the best properties for gathering and draping. However, even within that category, there are distinct differences in the way the papers perform. Able to handle the turquoise paper so remarkably like fabric, I had little difficulty pleating and gathering wide hemmed "flounces." To add color interest, I used three other papers in the outfit; one in gold colors that gives the impression of soft brocade, and the other in pink with tiny white flowers. The lovely white paper with distinctive lacy pattern was an amazing find as it not only drapes beautifully around the shoulders, but, by carefully tearing and cutting it, I could simulate lace trim at the bodice edges and wrist ruffles. Using a crafting tool for paper, I punched out flowers in pink and gold, alternating them in an undulating pattern around the hems of the three layers or "flounces." I glued a turquoise half bead, from the scrap-booking department, in each flower center.

PRETTY's fashion is unmistakably that of *c.*1850 during the reign of Queen Victoria, who ruled Britain from 1837 to 1901. The qualities of the paper and, yes, the bold turquoise color is perfect for the look. There is a mistaken tendency to romanticize Victorian fashion by assuming ladies dressed either in pastels or drab colors. Although ball gowns were white or pastel, and mourning clothes were black, strong colors were very popular for daywear and continued to be so in succeeding decades. The important elements of the period's outline consisted of a tight "bodice," tiny waist and skirt often with three or more horizontal rows of "flounces." The skirt's outline assumed a bell shape, achieved by gathering a surprisingly wide length of fabric into a very small waist circumference. To attain the correct silhouette, ladies required the use of several undergarment aids: a very tight corset for the upper body, and numerous "petticoats" and "crinolines" for the lower body. Wire hoops did not appear until later in the decade. To further enhance the impression of a petite torso with tiny waist, sleeves at the upper arm were tight, and the waist slightly lower. The "bodice" displays a series of pleats originating at the shoulder and ending at the waist like a *V* or fan shape, while pleat folds of the gold paper present a vertical line down the front, finished off with half-beads as buttons. The lower "bishop sleeves" are fully gathered and end tightly at the wrist.

Using smooth, shiny curling ribbon of paper, meant for curled gift package trim, I cut the lengths into narrow strips, and made tiny ringlets for the doll's hair. A ruffle of the white lacy paper frames her face, while the all-important "poke bonnet" of pink paper represents the crowning glory. Not as large as that of FLORAL EXUBERANCE, the bonnet is decorated in a much more restrained manner with the tiniest pink seed-like clusters, and several varieties of white paper flowers from a craft store's bridal section. A pleated "bavolet," or short curtain, appears at the back to cover her neck, while a large pink paper bow, whose edges I cut with decorative scissors, sits below the chin.

Giving her a dainty "reticule" (handbag) to carry is appropriate in conveying the prim and proper look of the day. The handle and edging are made of tightly wound paper to look like cording. I used the same technique to outline parts of the bodice and sleeve cuffs.

Constructing this paper creation for PRETTY IN PAPER was a delightful challenge. I deliberately put in details for any of you who might wish to try this method of doll dressing. I do, however, feel that knowing how to work with real fabrics is a basic prerequisite for achieving a successful result with paper.

Princess Caterina

Height: Lantern 14"
4.5" seated figure

In the year 2000, I created PRINCESS CATERINA. Having just given up my shop, I searched for a new direction in my doll making. I found it in the form of an adult figure, but with a twist; namely, with the face of a cat. I did not set out to make a whole series of cat dolls, but this concept kept inspiring me. Having spent the previous twenty years working exclusively in miniature, it is not surprising that the first of these creations would be in small scale.

Originally made to house a candle, this copper metal lantern took on a new life as a miniature room with silk drapes, tapestry carpeting, a gold bird cage with long metal tassel, and delicate climbing vines. Everything inside is in traditional miniature dollhouse scale of 1" to 1'. CATERINA enjoys her surroundings of comfort and luxury with a table set for tea and cake, while the court cat jester entertains her by dancing gracefully with a butterfly. In her paw, the princess holds a mirror to admire her appearance.

Working in small scale requires care not to engage in particulars that can overwhelm the figure, yet one needs to provide enough detail so as to be interesting. This costume harkens to the sixteenth century "Renaissance," but I exaggerated the sleeves with ample puffs in order to allow her pet bird to nestle in the soft silk folds. Trimmings include narrow white strips of fake fur, antique gold braid, and pearls, all characteristic of the time. The "stomacher" and robe's skirt are of the same fabric with a pattern suggesting brocade. A lace "ruff" around her neck fills in the upper chest area, while several long necklaces, reflecting the fashion of wealthy ladies, add jeweled interest.

The lantern's open door beckons the viewer to peek in on a tranquil interior scene befitting a royal feline, CATERINA.

Queen Bee

Height: 18"

During a trip to San Francisco, I lost myself in a famous fabric store, called Britex, and fell in love with two stunning fabrics. I was determined to use them together, but had no idea how. The beautiful quality of a striped silk with its unusual shade of yellow, caught my attention first, and, luckily, I found a solid material in a perfect match. Furthermore, the silk's sheen and the solid's matte finish complemented each other beautifully. The weave of the striped fabric mandated that the design be used horizontally, and the ideal inspiration arrived out of the proverbial nowhere: QUEEN BEE. Those horizontal stripes, in concert with contrasting black, were precisely the correct fit.

This costume is an amalgamation of style elements from various parts of eighteenth-century fashions. To give the rounded impression of a bee's middle, I hiked up and puffed out the striped material at the sides of the "overdress" in a fashion feature, reminiscent of "panniers," the French word for baskets. Commonly recognized as a prominent facet of 1700s costuming, "panniers" appeared in varying shapes, depending on the fashion of the time. The primary purpose of the metal or basketry hoop construction was to force the skirts out and away from the hips. Toward the 1770s, dresses reached a sideward spread of astonishing widths, but by the 1780s, as we see in CATBIRD, skirt widths had diminished considerably, leaving only a rounded protrusion in the back. By the 1790s, partially as a reaction to the tumultuous French Revolution, women adopted a simpler style of dress that hugged the body. The influence of "panniers," however, remains until today through such fashion terminology as "pannier"-draping, or "pannier"-like, when describing looped up skirt material. The QUEEN'S "overskirt" represents an elliptical hoop shape; the sides protrude while the front and back remain flat. Her gathered ankle length "underskirt" exposing heeled shoes, and the hairdo featuring masses of ringlets are inspired by the 1780s, as is the "caraco" black silk jacket. The decorated "stomacher" is a costume element of long-standing historical importance.

I purposely chose ribbons of black velvet to convey bee-like definition. As opposed to rayon or silk, velvet is denser, richer, and more color saturated, thereby rendering it especially effective in delineating sharp contrasts. I interspersed shiny drops of clear, glass beads with bold, black "venise" lace for the dramatic hem border. As she is a royal creature, I created a modified crown of silver "filigree" encircling a black silk pouf, with two antennae of glass flowers. Hanging rhinestones at the base of the "stomacher" come from an antique necklace I wore to my son's wedding and which are now on permanent display as a happy reminder. Wings of glittered organza nestle at her back.

Several bees appear as decoration: on the generous silver bows, her tail, and on the hand that gently brushes aside a wisp of hair in the same unusual yellow color as her dress.

A PICTURE OF ELEGANCE, IT IS EASY TO UNDERSTAND HOW THIS QUEEN BEE COMMANDS THE LOYALTY SHE RECEIVES FROM HER SUBJECTS, BE THEY BEES OR US.

Royal Bag Lady

Height: 17"

The ROYAL BAG LADY represents a doll I created specially for my Czech daughter-in-law, Nikol, to honor her as the family awaited the birth of her second son, and my second grandchild.

Although we are of different generations and nationalities, (I am American of British birth), she and I shared the same childhood passion. We both loved to draw make-believe pictures of beautiful princesses with gold crowns nestled atop long cascading blonde curls. Gowns with long, luxurious skirts, ample sleeves, ruffles and laces transported us each to a magical world of royal fantasy. In fact, royalty and crowns represent a recurring theme in many of the dolls contained in this book.

This princess, like Nikol, is an admirer of unusual purses and bags: The kitten peering out of the black velvet satchel adds a whimsical tribute to the impending birth.

Instead of replicating one historical period, I put together a composite of several fashions including some elements from the post-"Restoration" era in 1660. I paid particular attention to the skirt, for it provides the background against which to display the bags. As in this figure, mid-seventeenth century "overskirts" were gently pulled to the sides and held in place with substantial bows or "rosettes," to display an "underskirt" of different fabric. Ruffles of fabric or lace generally covered the skirt's lower edge. Full sleeves ended just past the elbow, while wide ribbon bows continued to adorn both dress and hair decoration. The tiered rows of lace bring to mind Victorian fashion of the 1850s, while the wide beaded band at the waist and lower arms do not denote any particular era, yet remain proportional and harmonious with the gown as a whole.

The plaid silk underskirt determines the color scheme of dusty red in the "overskirt" as well as the gold of the decorative hem. The border is limited to shades of gold so as not to detract from the colorful bags, which constitute a series of mini focal points. I topped two rows of ruffled gold "lamé" with a series of delicate branches of leaves snipped out from a larger trim, placing them on the "underskirt" at an angle. Soft green beads appear within the branches, adding sparkle. The strong colors of the purses make them stand out in contrast to the pale plaid skirt background. Beads, embroidery and mini applique embellish and enhance the various bags. What was a nondescript filigree holder for pills became the gilded bag seen hanging in front, now decorated with "ruched" ribbon, a tassel and beaded handle.

STEPPING OUT FROM THE PAGES OF THOSE LONG-AGO GIRLHOOD DRAWINGS BY TWO NOW-GROWNUP WOMEN, THIS PRINCESS, THE ROYAL BAG LADY, HAS A PERMANENT PLACE IN BOTH OUR LIVES.

Sitting on Top of the World

Height: 12" total
7" seated figure

For those of us who live with cats, there can be little doubt as to who is in charge of whom. This puppeteer demonstrates just who pulls the proverbial strings as he controls the dance steps of his two human puppets. I was inspired to create the white-haired, bespectacled doll maker immediately after seeing a stunning production of the ballet, *Coppelia*.

Drawn from eighteenth- to early nineteenth-century fashion, our well-dressed gentleman wears a three-piece ensemble of jacket, vest, and trousers, each in differing colors and fabrics. These three pieces of apparel set the basic and recognizable framework for men's suits until the present day, although there were many variations through the succeeding centuries. Here our puppeteer sports an open, floral, velvet jacket with what appears to be gold embroidery. In fact, the faux embroidery is the product of strategically attached gilded lace. A high collar and deep sleeve cuffs, ending in lace wrist ruffles, add appropriate finish. A buttoned silk vest repeats what appears to be gold embroidery on its pockets while contrasting braid serves to outline and give definition. In the back, the coat tails humorously flare out in tandem with the cat's tail. Jackets, at this time, were well constructed with precision fit, and the British, in particular, set the highest standard of expert tailoring to emulate. Until this time, men wore primarily "breeches," or pants ending at the knee over white silk stockings; however, at the beginning of the nineteenth century, trousers became fashionable, and remained so permanently. A silk bow and lace "jabot" fill in the neck.

The children wear clothing typical of the period; she in frothy pale blue chiffon and he in olive green silk.

Comfortably perched on the globe, looking down upon his prancing human charges, Sitting on Top the World leaves no question as to who has the final say.

MER

MER DU SUD ou PACIFIQUE
Equinoctiale
MER DU

Taming of the Shoe

Height: 14"

The trio of colors in this women's high-heeled shoe determined this costume's beautiful palette of chocolate brown "silk taffeta," verdant green velvety velour, and rich pink silk ribbons. The British "Restoration Period" (1660 through 1680s) was the initial inspiration for this figure, although the finished product is clearly fantasy. Heavy use of ornamentation prevailed especially in masculine attire of the time. It is precisely because male clothing was, by modern standards, so effeminate, that I took artistic liberties with hints of both sexes. In what we think of as a feminine feature, various shoe charms, featuring high heels, appear thematically throughout, including on the full, fluffy tail. The feet, which seem to be braking, sport real leather shoes with a fashionable heel. I topped the lace-trimmed, fully gathered pants with four heavily beaded panels, while pink bows and soft silk ruffles appear in the hat, sash, and the wrists. The hair, despite pink and green color accents is, nevertheless, in the style of an amply curled "periwig" worn by men. The headdress consists of a fussy concoction of leaves, laces, and ribbon flowers, topped off with a pair of painted metal shoe "findings" on the end of a spiraled wire. A wide range of textural components make up this costume, including silks, "velour," wool, embroidered cotton panels, beads, fur, and metal, all of which work together to produce different surface decoration.

Confidently holding on to a thin leather rein, astride the shoe as a vehicle, sits the finest example of a feline shoe tamer.

The Cat's Meow

Height: 16"

Dictionary definitions of the expression, CAT'S MEOW use words such as: a highly desired person or thing, outstanding, fabulous, and hot stuff. This theatrical lady incorporates all of these terms as she stretches out her arms in delight to receive her accolades. In selecting both the pose as well as the fashion to portray the doll's title, *The Merry Widow*, a light-hearted operetta, which premiered in 1905, came to mind, therefore the choice of costume from that era. During this the "Edwardian period," named after Edward VII, who ruled Britain from 1901 to 1910, women's fashion exhibited a lavish display of laces, dresses with trains, and large hats trimmed with feathers, florals, birds, and ribboning. To my mind, this period represents the beginning of the end of über feminine clothes which served very little other purpose than to make women exude a look of elegant grace, charm, and fine manners; in other words, the perfect decorative lady of leisure, like a twentieth-century interpretation of A LADY OF QUALITY. Such delicate attire for daytime wear would very soon disappear, to all intents and purposes, forever. Women had just begun to adopt clothing related to practical activities as they increasingly discovered the worlds of sports and employment.

In focusing on THE CAT'S MEOW, one cannot miss her elaborately adorned, over-the-top hat, which despite its exaggerated size, she manages to balance beautifully on her head, and on an angle no less!

The lavender color of her silk hat reappears in the trained dress, but with a very different fabric. Here the material has a definite texture owing to the tiniest clear beads woven throughout in a geometric pattern. As regards the coat-like "overdress," the shades of color appear to vary through a spectrum of bluish pink, rose, mauve, and purple depending on the direction of light. These various colors then repeat in the beading, flowers, and outlining.

The soft green of the hat's leaf stalks dictate the third color, without which the ensemble would have seemed incomplete and less interesting. Extending from one black-mittened hand to the other, the loosely draped silk shawl comprises an important element in unifying and pulling together the whole composition. As laces were so ubiquitous during this time, I made generous use of antique varieties in the "jabot," collar, sleeve ruffles, and the lower back of her dress.

A discussion of this fashion would be incomplete without mention of the era's silhouette. If not for the availability of clever and sophisticated corsetry, there would be no way a woman could have achieved the impossibly small waists we have come to associate with "Victorian" and early 1900s fashion. This figure displays the desired hourglass figure, called the "wasp-waist." Early in the twentieth century, fashion decreed a new silhouette outline, called the "S-bend," because women's posture resembled the letter S. To achieve that look, new corsets flattened the stomach while tilting the hips back; the mono-bosom, in turn, was thrust forward like the "pouter pigeon" look described in CATBIRD. Where women were not naturally endowed with the requisite body fullness, padding filled in the rest.

As she charmingly dangles her feather fan in one hand, this petite miss seems to be saying: Look at me, world! Am I not beautiful and captivating? In short and in every way, THE CAT'S MEOW.

The Doll Lady

Height: 19" total
14" seated figure

In my previous life, from 1977 through 1999, I owned and ran a shop, called The Doll Lady. Prior to that time, I had established a reputation as a doll maker, and customers who bought my creations at shows and fairs referred to me by that name. When I opened the store, my intent was to specialize in dolls, both factory-made as well as those I hand-made: hence the shop's name. Over the years, the business moved in another direction and I became a specialty store for Dollhouses and Miniatures. Although I no longer sold dolls, I could not bear to part with the name, and kept it. I may not have the store anymore, but the name and I have never parted company.

I always wanted to include, in this collection, a cat doll creating smaller dolls and toys, so when I found the decor item of an outsized spool of thread, I knew I had the right beginning. It is the perfect scale for my preferred doll size (approximately 14"-18" tall, standing), and around which to display a selection of favorite miniatures I had accumulated over the years. Foreseeing a busy composition, this working lady's dress needed to be less extravagant than the others in the series so as not to compete with the collection of miniatures surrounding her perch. At the same time, I meant for the doll maker to remain the primary focus, which is why I deliberately chose to employ strong colors both for the basic outfit as well as the complementary accents.

In the late 1700s, a bonnet-like head covering for women, called a "mob-cap," became relatively ubiquitous, and varied in design. Certain characteristics, however, were intrinsic to most of them – a full, high, gathered or pleated pouf of a crown, edged with ruffles or gathers, and frequently surrounded by a band of ribbon where the pouf met the gathers. In order to make the cap the doll's most prominent costume feature, I exaggerated the size, and chose a bright chartreuse green "silk taffeta" for the fabric. Silk ribbon in deep pink, form into soft, generous loops, simulating a large "rosette," while lace ruffles and tight hair curls, characteristic of the 1780s (see CATBIRD), flatteringly frame her spectacled face.

I adopted the same bright green in the silk cap for the dress, but, instead, used cotton fabric with a subtle pattern. Along the full skirt's hem, rich purple silk ribbon, strategically caught up in soft evenly spaced bunches, creates a striking color and textural contrast. The long fitted jacket is called a "caraco." It represents an informal clothing style dating from the 1760s, increasing in popularity through the 1780s, and considered an appropriate fashion for working women. I trimmed the strong purple "caraco" with lace, purple beads and a splash of bright yellow woven flowers, while repeating this unexpected color on the upper sleeves and cap. She wears a "fichu" scarf of antique lace around her shoulders.

Miniature scissors, spools of thread, a dangling tape measure, and a partially finished stuffed rabbit in her lap, all contribute to illustrating her profession as a doll and toy maker. I dressed the small doll, placed beneath her demurely crossed feet, in a matching outfit.

Names of some of the manufacturers of the miniatures shown include: Deb Canham, Hantel, Ann Anderson and World of Miniature Bears.

Thinking Outside the Box

Height: 12" total
10" seated figure

In order to illustrate this now iconic phrase, I looked to the sixteenth century for my initial inspiration, while fantasy determined the end result. The pattern of the Italian Florentine wrapping paper I used to cover the box, has a decidedly "Renaissance" look, and the large brass ornaments bring to mind a "Tudor rose." The deep, cool blue color of the paper background acts as a counterweight to the vibrant, almost neon orange and hot pink silk colors in the dress. The florid design of the paper and the solid colors of the dress, effectively, play off each other. Insertion of an old, nearly greenish shade of gold acts as a bridge between what may appear to be two contradictory concepts. That is, the bright and exuberant dress shades have a modern feel, yet, the burnished gold threads, the embroidery on the front bodice and aged metal trims suggest antiquity. Old gold reappears not only in beaded embellishments, but also as the pronounced fringe-like edging of the fabric petticoat, playfully peeking out below her pink skirt and at the sleeve ends. I used upholstery trim to construct the curly hair, and added shiny highlights of spirals fashioned from gold wire. Her high-standing collar is a loose translation of a "whisk," trimmed at the points with "findings." The doll's sitting position determines the overall dress design, whereby the skirt drapes and falls in such a way as to keep the delicate lace booties and gold stockinged legs clearly visible. Coordinating flowers, made of tiny "yo-yo circles," nestle in clusters among the skirt's generous folds.

Artfully poised on her proverbial thinking box, this dainty miss, THINKING OUTSIDE THE BOX, strikes a fetching image of dreamy reverie.

Walk on the Wild Side

Height: 17"

The mid 1880s presents the costumer with an endless and exciting array of possibilities to pull out all the proverbial stops of dress creation, thanks to the evolution of the dramatic "bustle." Aided by a rounded undergarment contraption of basketry, metal, and/or wire, the "bustle" grew through the early 1880s until it reached its most extreme perch-like protrusion in 1885, before gradually declining in size through the remainder of the decade. "Overskirts" were pulled to the rear, and festooned up and back into something resembling a shelf. This focal point, then, afforded the dressmaker a unique foundation upon which to create all manner of cascades, bunching, and ever more exaggerated and complicated draping. Seamstresses used their considerable skills to tastefully attach every imaginable form of trim and decoration, Severe boned corsetry created the rigidly tight bodice with accompanying tiny waist, hallmarks essential to achieve the distinctive silhouette. Highly tailored jackets of walking outfits generally came to a low point in front, frequently including "revers" or lapels, lace or gathered "plastrons" (front bodice panels), military style high collars edged with gathered lace, and fitted cuffed sleeves.

Brimmed hats, often in the shape of an inverted flower pot, represented a popular style, while ladies wore their upswept hair close to the head with some tight curls at the forehead and nape of the neck.

The slim, close-to-the-body fashion of the upper torso stood in marked contrast to the generous massing of fabrics in the skirt. Multiple layers of skirts created an abundance of interest thereby commanding the most attention. The "underskirt" comprised the first layer, partially covered by one or more draped panels, called "apron" fronts.

Our elegantly bedecked lady, walking her pet lion, exemplifies the epitome of this fashion period. Incorporating the necessary assortment of ruffles, pleats, bows, ribbons, laces, flowers, tassels, fringes, braids, and beads is essential. I began by selecting three fabric colors to repeat throughout the outfit: grayish green silk taffeta, dusty rose "dupioni" silk, and a cotton print in varying shades of greens and pinks. The cotton works in concert with the silks, because beautiful accents of bright metallic gold enrich the fabric's paisley pattern.

I constructed the doll to be seen from a side angle, so as to present the viewer with as much of the skirt detail as possible. The whole front section of the skirt consists of three separate layers. I combined delicate antique lace with the rose silk, pleating the two pieces together as a single fabric for the first layer. The second, of green "silk taffeta," introduces an "apron front" trimmed with ribbon "rosettes," dipping down softly over the "underskirt." The paisley cotton, which represents the top layer, has sharp-edged pleats, designed to contrast with the gentle folds of the underlying "apron." The all-important skirt back also consists of three components, with the green silk resting between two cotton layers. As cotton fabric does not behave the same way as silk, it became necessary to compensate for its inability to hold the desired drape formations on its own. While shaping the fabric, I used invisible stitches to permanently hold the formations in place so as to convey the effect of elaborate folds and draping on the "bustle" top and down the back. Among the varieties of embellishments, I included "ruched" ribbon, braiding, beading, bows, and tassels, composed of gold "findings" strung together. In one leather-gloved hand, she holds a matching bag with a sweet antique button for accent. In the other, she is holding the lion's gold and pearl leash, which is a family heirloom necklace no longer worn, but now forever on display. Her gold necklace is my bracelet and the brooch an antique piece with just the right coloring. I came across the lion at an antique show many years ago, and saved it to use for the perfect inspiration.

SOME MIGHT DISMISS THE EXCESSES OF DECORATION AND EMBELLISHMENT SO CHARACTERISTIC OF THIS PERIOD AS FRIPPERY. I CALL IT STRIKING!

Zelda

Height: 17"

Representing the last doll in this thirty-one-piece cat-doll collection, I created ZELDA with a special purpose: to demonstrate how it is possible to create a successful historical costume from your local fabric and craft stores. Not everyone has the luxury of living within a reasonable distance from world famous fabric districts, and yet that does not need, by any means, to be a deterrent. I am not being paid by Jo-Ann to advertise for them: In fact, they have no idea I am doing this. Nevertheless, it is a fact that they are dominant and well known with stores in every state, and many of us rely on their presence for our sewing needs, including me. I am impressed with the breadth of their reasonably priced fabric choices, and with each new project requiring different needs, I see merchandise as if for the first time, regardless of how long it may have been in the store.

Having no preconceived notion of what I would create, I wondered the aisles with a free and open mind. The material to speak to me first was one I had never before considered for a historical doll: denim! A soft, lightweight denim fabric in traditional dark blue and with a subtle iridescent surface became my new inspirational starting point. Not yet sure of the costume plan, I also purchased the same fabric in pale blue denim, although, I ended up not using it. Three other materials emerged as ideal complements. First, I selected a blue and white stripe fabric that feels and looks remarkably like silk "charmeuse," although it is polyester. Its soft sheen is important as it adds a texture that is completely different from the others. Second, a two-tone small print of light and blue cotton fits well with the first two choices, both in color and design. The third accent fabric is a lightweight "silk taffeta" in deep, pink fuschia, which I had already used in THINKING OUTSIDE THE BOX, but with strikingly different color combinations. This hot pink silk turned out to be the critical, dramatic element to pull the whole ensemble together, although I had no idea that would be the case when I purchased it. Initially, I imagined it as a strong, but relatively small, accent point in the finished result.

After searching through my library of fashion and costume books for an appropriate period that I had not yet tackled, I selected *c.*1889. There is a tendency to underestimate the changes that took place during "the Victorian Era," by lumping a decade or even several decades together to try to epitomize certain fashion characteristics. However, even within each decade, there were often huge changes. As a cursory example, during the 1880s, skirts still gave a narrow appearance in the front, while the back "bustle" went from a slight protrusion to jaw-dropping extremes (see WALK ON THE WILD SIDE). Remaining in fashion for only a few years, it then declined sharply to a pale shadow of itself by 1890. As the 1890s began, the skirts became bell-shaped and "bustles" disappeared. Sleeves, straight and tight in the 1880s, began to expand in the early 1890s, growing to huge "leg-of-mutton" proportions by the mid-decade (see CAT IN A HAT). The style lasted only for a short time, and with the approach of the twentieth century, sleeves again became slender. The choice, then, of *c.*1889 represents a point midway between two examples of fashion extremes.

Under ZELDA's slender blue skirt, I created an "underskirt" of the blue/white "charmeuse." The stripes themselves, if left untreated, were too wide for the size of the figure. With soft pleats, I camouflaged the fabric into the appearance of narrower stripes, and thereby maintained the necessary scale. Tight corsetry of the earlier decade continued to force the torso into impossibly small waists, as ZELDA's bodice demonstrates. Sleeve gathers, particularly at the shoulders, are just the beginning of what will develop into the oversized shape to come, while the high neckline remains unchanged. The printed cotton appears as a tailored blouse and "reticule." Unable to resist letting the beautiful "silk taffeta" do what it does best, i.e., hold a draped shape, I formed the suggestion of a "bustle" and a train, adorning its edge with silver braid, and, almost magically, found ribbon flowers to match the hot pink silk. The use of silver for most of the trimmings picks up the denim's silvery sheen, and although trains continued into the 1890s, I exercised artistic license in making it so prominent. The introduction of stark white "venise" laces affords a visual break from the stronger costume colors. I used pink and metallic blue beads of differing sizes for shine and fringing.

I topped her upswept wavy hair and front curls with a fussy bonnet of ruffles and flowers, while ribbons tie in a bow under the chin.

By sharing the creative journey described above, I hope to inspire others to experiment with unexpected fabrics and combinations. I can only say, if others get as much enjoyment out of a project as I did this one, you will be well rewarded.

ZELDA MAY BE LAST IN ALPHABETICAL LISTING; HOWEVER, WHEN IT COMES TO FINE DRESSING, SHE HOLDS HER OWN WITH THE REST OF THIS VOLUME'S PRESENTERS.

Glossary of Terms

The Glossary contains all words and terminology appearing within quotation marks in the written texts.

Apollo Knot

An artificial hair piece affixed to the top of the head and decorated with a variety of trims and/ or feathers. Particularly for evening wear in the 1830s. May include braided and looped hair.

Apron Front or Panel

Also known by the French translation, "tablier." Represents a layer of fabric draping on top of an "underskirt" that resembles an apron. It was particularly prominent as a fashion feature in the 1870s and 1880s.

Art Deco

An eclectic, artistic, and design style originating in the 1920s in Paris and extremely popular internationally throughout the 1930s. The style influenced all areas of design, including architecture, interior and industrial design, fashion, and jewelry, as well as the visual arts, such as painting, graphic arts, and film.

Bavolet

A ruffled or pleated curtain at the back of a bonnet, designed to protect the neck.

Betsie

An imitation of the "ruff," popularly worn during the "Elizabethan Era." The name is a diminutive of Elizabeth.

Bishop Sleeve

A long sleeve, fuller at the bottom than the top, gathered at the wrist, and ending with a cuff or ruffle.

Bloody Mary

Queen Mary I, and daughter of King Henry VIII and Catherine of Aragon, who became Queen of England in 1553 upon the death of her young brother, Edward VI, a Protestant. Despite Henry's break with the Catholic Church, Mary returned the country to Catholicism. She arranged the murders of hundreds of dissenters, earning her the name, "Bloody Mary." Upon her death, Elizabeth assumed the throne and reestablished Protestantism. Not to be confused with Mary, Queen of Scots.

Bodice

The upper part of a woman's dress, from shoulders to waist.

Breeches

A general word for numerous styles of short pants extending from waist to knee. Styles range from narrow to very wide, depending on time line.

Bum Roll

A padded, crescent-shaped pillow worn just below the waist, under a woman's skirt to force it outwards, away from the body. Made the hips seem wider, while making the waist appear smaller. Worn primarily from sixteenth through eighteenth centuries. Sometimes referred to as "hip roll."

Bustle

A framework of metal or whalebone designed to expand the skirt's fullness or support its draping in the back. Worn in back below the waist, it was popular during the later part of the "Victorian Era."

Canions (also Canons)

Tubular-shaped upper stockings, often embroidered, ending at the knee. Generally attached to "trunk hose."

Caraco

A fitted style of jacket with tight upper or long sleeves often used by working women or as casual wear. Especially popular from the 1760s through 1780s

Cavalier Collar

Also called falling band or Van Dyke collar, after the artist. Worn in the seventeenth century, a lace or lace-edged collar falling gracefully upon the shoulders.

Charmeuse

Light weight, silk or polyester fabric with a smooth satin finish on one side, and dull finish on the other. Its slinky softness makes it challenging to work with.

Chatelaine

Chain worn at the waist, used for holding a wide variety of items such as keys, watch, purse, useful trinkets, etc.

Copella

Ballet composed by Delibes in 1870. About an inventor, Dr. Coppelius, who creates a life-sized dancing doll.

Crinoline

Horsehair, cotton or linen material were used to make these stiffened petticoats from 1840s. Used to support many petticoats under ever increasing skirt widths. The weight of numerous petticoats and crinolines led to the use of metal hoops by the late 1850s.

De Riguer

Required by the current custom or fashion. The expression is French meaning rigor or strictness.

Dernier Cri

Refers to the latest fashion. The expression is French translating as last or latest cry.

Dolman Sleeve

Very full and wide at the armhole and narrow at the wrist.

Doublet

A man's snug-fitting buttoned jacket worn from the late fourteenth to the mid seventeenth century, especially during the "Renaissance Period." Sometimes edged at the waist with a series of tabs, possibly a vestige of doublet skirts, worn earlier, and which also lay on top of the "breeches" below.

Duponi

Medium weight silk fabric from India with a slight sheen and distinctive irregular, random slubs in the weave. Available in huge range of solid colors and sometimes patterns. Has a crunchable quality, allowing the fabric to hold folds.

Edwardian Era

Technically, refers to the years of British King Edward VII reign. He succeeded his mother, Queen Victoria, upon her death in 1901, and ruled until his death in 1910. The term is often used to describe the historical period between 1901 and 1919, after the end of WWI.

Elizabethan Era

Named after Elizabeth I, daughter of Henry VIII and Anne Boleyn. She succeeded her half sister, "Bloody Mary," and ruled from 1558 until her death in 1603.

Epaulet

Technically, an ornamental fringed shoulder pad, worn as part of a military uniform. I also use the term loosely to describe selected shoulder decorations.

Erté

Born Romain de Tirtoff (1892 - 1990), a Russian-born French artist, known by the pseudonym Erté, the French pronunciation of his initials, R.T. Major influence on "Art Deco," he designed for theater, film, graphic arts, fashion, and costume. Associated with *Harper's Bazar* (spelled then with one *a*) from 1915 -1936.

Farthingale

Circular hoop(s) designed to support and expand a gown's skirt horizontally from the waist. It was primarily a European fashion dominant in the sixteenth and early seventeenth centuries.

Fichu

A soft scarf, usually white, often triangular in shape, and worn like a shawl around the shoulders to cover a low round dress neckline.

Filigree

Ornamental, delicate, and intricate work of gold, silver or any fine twisted wire.

Findings

Small parts used both for jewelry making and many arts and crafts projects. Include beads and stamped metal pieces of enormous variety and shape.

Flounce

A wide or deep ruffle. Gathered or pleated fabric, lace or ribbon is attached at one lengthwise edge onto a garment.

Fontange

A tall lace/ribbon headdress popular in late seventeenth century. Aided by a wire structure, often achieving fantastic heights, it was worn at a forward tilt and attached to a cap. Usually included lappets.

French Hood

Generally associated with "Tudor" fashion, although it originated in France. Consisted of a stiffened, crescent-shaped headdress, often heavily jeweled, especially around the outlines. A fabric construction with a tubular design, hung in back, to contain the lady's hair.

Gores (also Godets)

Triangular shaped fabric pieces, inserted into a slash or seam, designed to give extra fullness to a garment, particular the skirt.

Harper's Bazar

A women's publication, which began in 1867 with the above spelling. Later on, the spelling changed to *Bazaar*.

Hanging Sleeves

Strips of fabric hanging from the shoulder.

Hobble Skirt

Pre-WWI style skirt so narrow, the wearer could only hobble with tiny steps.

Jabot

Ornamental cascade of lace or fabric frills appearing down the front of a shirt, blouse, or dress.

Lamé

Fabric woven with silver or gold metal threads, that create a metallic sheen. Used for solid surfaces or brocade design.

Lappets

Flap of fabric or lace attached to the back of certain period headdresses and designed to hang down over the shoulder.

Leg-of-Mutton Sleeve (also Gigot)

A huge, ballooning sleeve, resembling the shape of a leg of mutton, which tapers from large at top to narrow at bottom end.

Minaret Tunic (also Lampshade Tunic)

A short, circular skirt, layered on top of a "hobble" or "peg-top" skirt, it is designed to flare away from the body.

Mob-Cap

Large bonnet/cap with puffy crown and frilled or ruffled brim. Popularized in England toward the end of the eighteenth century.

Nether-Stocks (also Nether-Hose)

An old term for stockings, particularly referring to the lower section of stockings between the knee and foot.

Overskirt

In historical fashion, refers to the top skirt layer. Generally open in front to reveal part of the underskirt in the shape of a narrow or wide triangle.

Panniers or Paniers

From the French word for baskets. They were side basket hoop-like forms worn, during much of the eighteenth century, under skirts and tied to the waist. Designed to extend skirt widths at the sides. During the 1770s, widths reached their extremes.

Peg-Top Skirt

Similar to the "hobble skirt," but fuller at the hips.

Pelisse

A type of overcoat, of the early nineteenth century, following the lines of dress shapes, with a high waist and of varying lengths. During different periods in fashion history, the term, "pelisse," can refer to other shapes and styles.

Periwig (also Peruke)

A wig, worn by a man during the seventeenth and eighteenth centuries, it was composed of masses of curls, and could be large in overall size.

Petticoat

See: "Underskirt."

Petticoat Breeches

Worn from 1650s through early 1660s. Voluminous men's breeches, the bottom left ungathered so as to give the impression of a woman's petticoat.

Picot

Tiny loops on one or both edges of ribbon, braid or lace.

Pinked

The series of *V*s at a fabric's edge, created by special scissors, called pinking shears.

Plastron

A panel on the front of a tunic or bodice usually of a different color.

Pole Bonnet

So called because all one's hair could be poked inside. Came into fashion in the early 1800s. The brim projected around the face to shield the wearer from the elements. Held on the head by ribbons then tied in a bow under the chin.

Pomander

Small, perforated, gold or silver case hanging from a belt or neck-chain. Designed to contain or hold small receptacles of scented herbs or perfume. Used from late Middle Ages through seventeenth century.

Pouter Pigeon

Named after a breed of pigeons that expands its crop, (anatomical term for an area in the chest wall to store food), until it becomes enlarged. Used to describe a silhouette with puffed-out chest and sometimes protruding rear.

Renaissance Period

A time of cultural rebirth, originating in Italy, and spreading through Europe and Britain from late fourteenth through early seventeenth centuries. In Britain, the Renaissance dates from roughly early 1500s to early 1600s.

Restoration Period

Refers to the restoration of the British monarchy under Charles II in 1660. Some apply the term to the event itself, while others to the period following that event.

Reticule

Dainty, little handbag.

Revers

Generally refers to the lapel of a garment, or the underside of a turned-back lapel. Derives from French, meaning reverse.

Robe à L'Angelaise

Popular in the 1780s, an overdress or coat, with fitted bodice, collar, and low neckline worn with a "fichu." Relatively plain, the skirt was long and full.

Rosette

A design with many uses. For costume purposes, refers to a rose design made by gathered ribbon or silk.

Ruching

Tightly gathered or ruffled ribbon or fabric.

Ruff

Standing, pleated collar of varying sizes and shapes. Popularly worn during the "Renaissance Period." Made of starched linen or lace, and worn by men, women, and children.

S-Bend or S-Shape

Special corsetry forced the front upper torso to lean forward while, simultaneously, thrusting the hips toward the back, to give the impression of the letter *S*.

Silk Taffeta

Pure silk fabric with a polished, somewhat shiny surface. Even more than "dupioni" silk, taffeta's crisp finish allows the fabric to hold form and folds beautifully, and is considered a more formal fabric.

Slouch

A fashionable body posture, associated with the years just before and after 1920. Hips thrust forward, and drooped shoulders, along with flattened bosoms, created a sought-after look that obscured female curves.

Stomacher

A decorated *V*-shaped panel, usually stiffened, and worn over the chest and stomach. Designed to fill in the front opening of a woman's gown.

The Merry Widow

An extremely popular, light-hearted operetta, written by Franz Lehar, and introduced in 1905 in Vienna. Widely performed around the world.

Trunk Hose

An old term for "breeches" or knickers, and worn over hose or stockings. Popular in sixteenth and seventeenth century men's fashion, they were puffed or padded, reaching to the thigh or knee.

Tudor Period

Relates uniquely to English history from 1485 until 1603. The House of Tudor began with King Henry VII (father of Henry VIII), and ended with the death of Queen Elizabeth I. The Stuart line, beginning with James I, then ascended to the monarchy.

Tudor Rose

When Henry VII assumed the throne, he adopted the red and white rose as the Tudor emblem (symbolic of his win in the War of the Roses and the unification of the two warring houses). The design of the "Tudor Rose" remains the official floral emblem of Britain.

Tulle

Very fine netting of silk, rayon or nylon, and often starched. Commonly used for bridal veils, ballet tutus, and gowns.

Underskirt or Petticoat

In historical fashion, refers to a separate skirt worn with a bodice or gown under an overskirt. Meant to be visible and often elaborately embellished, unlike modern petticoats, which remain unseen.

Velour

A pliable, stretchy plush knit fabric, usually made of synthetic material.

Venise Lace (also Venice or Venetian Lace)

Heavier weight, often shiny surfaced, with floral or geometric designs connected to each other by bars of thread.

Victorian Era

Refers to the long reign of Queen Victoria, who ruled England from 1837 until 1901.

Virago Sleeve

Very full sleeves gathered above the elbow into two puffs either by ribbon or cording. Worn by women during the 1620s and 1630s.

Wasp-Waist

A stylish woman aimed for a 16-18" waist. Through the use of bone or metal strips and the tightest possible lacing of corsets, the look of the waist simulated the segmented body of a wasp.

Whisk Collar

A standing, semi-circular, and fan-shaped collar, made of lace or lace-edged material and worn by both men and women.

Yo-Yo Circles

Often used in quilting or applique. Created by gathering a circle twice the size of the desired finished size. By pulling the thread tight, fabric folds in on itself, thereby creating a lined pleated circle. The center may be embellished with beads or embroidery.

Selected Bibliography

The following list constitutes a selection of the books I found most important and useful for both research and inspiration, while assembling the subject matter of this volume. They are, by no means, the only reference books in my personal library or that are available on the subject of historical costume and fashion. All books are written in English, unless otherwise noted.

Arnold, Janet. *Patterns of Fashion 1: Englishwomen's Dresses and Their Construction c.1660-1860.* London, Great Britain: Macmillan Publishers Ltd., 1977.

Arnold, Janet. *Patterns of Fashion 2: Englishwomen's Dresses and Their Construction c.1860-1940.* London, Great Britain: Macmillan Publishers Ltd., 1977.

Arnold, Janet. *Patterns of Fashion: The Cut and Construction of Clothes for Men and Women c.1560-1620.* London, Great Britain: Macmillan Publishers Ltd., 1985.

Blum, Stella. *Ackermann's Costume Plates: Women's Fashions in England 1818-1828.* New York, New York: Dover Publications, Inc., 1978.

Blum, Stella. *Eighteenth-Century French Fashion Plates in Full Color.* New York, New York: Dover Publications, Inc., 1982.

Blum, Stella. *Victorian Fashions and Costumes From Harper's Bazar: 1867-1898.* New York, New York: Dover Publications, Inc., 1974.

Cunnington, C. Willett. *English Women's Clothing in the Nineteenth Century: A Comprehensive Guide with 1,117 Illustrations.* Mineola, New York: Dover Publications, Inc., 1990.

Erté. *Erté's Fashion Designs: 218 Illustrations from Harper's Bazar. 1918-1932.* Mineola, New York: Dover Publications, Inc., 1981.

Erté. *Fashion Drawings and Illustrations from Harper's Bazar.* Mineola, New York: Dover Publications, Inc., 1976.

Fukai, Akiko. *Fashion: The Collection of the Kyoto Costume Institute: A History from the 18th to the 20th Century.* New York, New York: Barnes and Noble, Inc., 2006.

Hill, Margot Hamilton and Bucknell, Peter A. *The Evolution of Fashion: Pattern and Cut from 1066 to 1930.* London, Great Britain: B.T. Batsford, Ltd., 1967.

Laver, James. *Costume and Fashion: A Concise History.* New York, New York: Thames and Hudson Inc., 1985

Laver, James. *Costume Through the Ages: 1000 Illustrations.* New York, New York: Simon and Schuster. 1963.

Leniston, Florence. *La Mode Illustrée: Fashion Plates in Full Color.* Mineola, New York: Dover Publications, Inc., 1997.

Luerti, Angelo. *Non Solo Erté: NotOonly Erté: Costume Design for the Paris Music Hall 1918-194.* Schio (Vicenza), Italy: Guido Tamoni Editore. 2006. Written in both Italian and English.

Peacock, John. *Costume 1066-1990s.* New York, New York: Thames and Hudson Ltd., 1986

Rothstein, Natalie. *Four Hundred Years of Fashion.* London, Great Britain: V&A Publications. 1984.

Shead, Richard. *Ballet Russes.* New York: Knickerbocker Press. 1998.

Wilcox, R. Turner. *The Dictionary of Costume.* New York, New York: Charles Scribner's Sons. 1969.

Wilcox, R. Turner. *The Mode of Costume.* New York, New York: Charles Scribner's Sons. 1958.

Yarwood, Doreen. *English Costume: From the Second Century B.C. to 1967.* London, Great Britain: B.T. Batsford. Ltd. 1967.

Yarwood, Doreen. *European Costume: 4000 Years of Fashion.* New York, New York: Bonanza Books, 1982.

Yarwood, Doreen. *The Encyclopedia of World Costume.* London, Great Britain: B.T. Batsford Ltd., 1978.